T0248218

A SECOND CHANCE

Also by Frederic Block

Crimes and Punishments

Race to Judgment

Disrobed

A SECOND CHANCE

A FEDERAL JUDGE DECIDES
WHO DESERVES IT

JUDGE FREDERIC BLOCK

NEW YORK
LONDON

Requests for permission to reproduce selections from this book should be made through our website: https://thenewpress.com/contact.

Published in the United States by The New Press, New York, 2024
Distributed by Two Rivers Distribution

LIBRARY OF CONGRESS CATALOGING-IN-PUBLICATION DATA

Names: Block, Frederic, 1934- author.
Title: A second chance : a federal judge decides who deserves it / Frederic Block.
Description: New York : The New Press, 2024. | Includes bibliographical references.
Identifiers: LCCN 2024015297 | ISBN 9781620978870 (hardcover) | ISBN 9781620979006 (ebook)
Subjects: LCSH: Judicial process--United States. | Judicial process--United States--Cases. | Law--United States--Decision making. | Criminal procedure--United States. | Criminal justice, Administration of--United States.
Classification: LCC KF8700 .B53 2024 | DDC 347.73/225--dc23/eng/20240409
LC record available at https://lccn.loc.gov/2024015297

The New Press publishes books that promote and enrich public discussion and understanding of the issues vital to our democracy and to a more equitable world. These books are made possible by the enthusiasm of our readers; the support of a committed group of donors, large and small; the collaboration of our many partners in the independent media and the not-for-profit sector; booksellers, who often hand-sell New Press books; librarians; and above all by our authors.

www.thenewpress.com

Composition by Bookbright Media
This book was set in Adobe Caslon and Helvetica Neue

Printed in the United States of America

10 9 8 7 6 5 4 3 2 1

This book is dedicated to Stephen May
and all others who deserve a second chance.

CONTENTS

A SECOND CHANCE

INTRODUCTION

I am a federal judge. On June 2, 2023, I let a murderer serving a lifetime sentence out of jail. Instead of dying in prison, he was now a free man.

The next day, I was vilified on the front page of the *New York Daily News*. I subsequently let other condemned men serving lifetime sentences out of jail. Why did I do that? Was it time for me, after serving twenty-nine years as a judge, to retire? Or was it the right thing to do?

A few years ago, Congress enacted a bipartisan sentencing-reform bill called the First Step Act. Among its sweeping provisions was one allowing a federal district judge—like me—to reconsider the appropriateness of a previously imposed sentence and to reduce that sentence, even if the original sentence was lawful. The act went so far as to allow the judge to nullify a lifetime sentence and grant the prisoner his freedom—as I have done. Never had such power been granted to a federal judge. As of January 2024, 4,680 federal inmates have been released by federal district judges since the act's creation.[1] There will be many more by the time this book is published. It has changed the whole concept and landscape of sentencing in the federal courts, recognizing that condemned prisoners may be entitled to a second chance. And it has motivated me to write this book.

The United States has the largest prison population percentage-wise of any country in the world. It has about 4% of the world's population but around 22% of the world's inmates.[2] About 1.9 million people out of the current U.S. population of about 330 million are incarcerated.[3] The alumni population is, of course, much larger. An August 2021 article in the *Harvard Political Review* reported that "[e]ach year, more than 600,000 individuals are released from state and federal prisons" and "[a]nother nine million are released from local jails."[4] It costs us over $80 billion a year to jail this population and to supervise former inmates when they are on post-incarceration supervised release.[5]

More shocking, as the article reports, "[w]ithin three years of their release, two out of three former prisoners are rearrested and more than 50% are incarcerated again."[6] But according to a report from the Sentencing Project—a nonpartisan Washington, DC–based research and advocacy center—over a three-year period after the First Step Act was enacted, the recidivism rate among those released from prison as a result of the act was only 12%, compared with 45% for the general prison population.[7]

On March 14, 2023, the Prison Policy Initiative, an independent research and national criminal justice reform advocacy organization, reported that "[at] least 113 million adults in the U.S. (roughly 45%) have a family member who has been incarcerated, and 79 million people have a criminal record, revealing the ripple effects of locking up millions of people every day." The report also confirmed that "people of color—who face much greater rates of poverty—

are dramatically overrepresented in the nation's prisons and jails." Although books have been written by criminologists, sociologists, and psychologists explaining the reasons for this, the stark reality, as the report points out, is that Black Americans make up 38% of the incarcerated population although they represent only 12% of U.S. residents.[8]

We truly have a mass incarceration problem.

But most of the jail population comes from the states. Federal prisoners constitute about two hundred thousand of the inmates, or roughly 10% of our total prison population. State prisons and local jails house the other roughly 90%, and currently only a handful of states—including California, Colorado, New Jersey, Pennsylvania, and Ohio—and the District of Columbia allow prisoners to petition a state court judge for release under limited circumstances.[9] However, there has been some minimum momentum to pass "Second Look" bills in the states, and, as of writing, some states, including New York, are considering enacting legislation.

The idea of letting a criminal out of jail before his full sentence has been served is politically charged. Arkansas Republican senator Tom Cotton has blamed the First Step Act for making America "less safe." He believes that "[i]f anything, we have an under-incarceration problem" and has referred to the First Step Act as "criminal leniency legislation."[10] Former vice president Mike Pence believes that "[n]ow more than ever, we ought to be thinking about how we make penalties tougher on people that are victimizing families in this country." And Florida governor Ron DeSantis, who sought the Republican nomination for president, had called the act "basically, a jailbreak bill" that has "allowed dangerous people out of prison." If he had become president, one of the first things he would have done was "to go to Congress and seek the repeal of the First Step Act."[11]

I am a huge supporter of the First Step Act's reforms. So is

Justice Neil Gorsuch of the United States Supreme Court, who in a recent dissent wrote that the First Step Act "may be the most significant criminal justice reform bill in a generation."[12] I especially embrace that part of the act that gives me the discretion to reconsider a previously imposed sentence. I believe in the biblical concept of redemption and that the First Step Act appropriately provides a path to allow a worthy prisoner a second chance to live a law-abiding life.

But what about the roughly 90% of the prison and jail population serving state sentences? Logic dictates that they should also be given the same opportunity at a second chance that the First Step Act now gives the federal prisoner. But, as we shall see, they are not. I argue in this book that the states should follow the federal lead and enact legislation similar to the First Step Act.

I'm often asked to explain the differences between criminal cases that are handled in federal courts and those that are tried in state courts. Under the Tenth Amendment, each state has the power to enact its own criminal laws and to mete out punishment to those who violate those state laws. The laws run the gamut from domestic violence to murder, but the crimes must be committed within the state. They are called *intrastate* crimes.

By contrast, Congress decides which acts constitute federal crimes. If they cross state lines, they are known as *interstate* crimes. For example, a murder committed solely within a state under a state's murder statute can be prosecuted only in that particular state. But if the murder is in aid of racketeering—which often traverses state boundaries—it can be prosecuted in federal court. The same is true of drug and gun crimes. Congress has declared that drugs travel in interstate commerce, and guns invariably have components manufactured in different states.

In addition, some crimes are purely federal. If a federal officer were murdered, that would be a federal crime. Other examples of interstate federal crimes include terrorism, bank robbery, federal income tax evasion, mail and wire fraud, and possession, receipt, or promotion via the internet of child pornography.

Of course, a crime can be both a federal and a state crime. For example, states have their own drug laws that often mirror the federal drug laws. In those cases, the federal and state prosecutors where the crime has been committed will usually meet and decide whether the crime will be prosecuted in state or federal court. The feds have the first option. They will decide if the crime is sufficiently serious that it should be "federalized." It makes a big difference, because federal penalties are invariably higher than state penalties.

Recent statistics released by the National Center for Drug Abuse reveal that 46% of prisoners in federal prison and 26% of women and 13% of men in state prisons are there for drug-related crimes.[13] Approximately 57% of people incarcerated in state prison and 77% of people incarcerated in federal prison for drug offenses are Black or Latino, while those two groups together account for only a little over 30% of the U.S. population.[14]

I'm also often asked to explain the difference between federal and state sentencing. Under federal law, the sentencing judge must impose a fixed sentence and there is no parole. The prisoner must serve the entire sentence but may be given 15% credit for good behavior. The Federal Bureau of Prisons makes the good behavior determination, which is not subject to judicial review. Until the First Step Act was passed, the district judge had a limited role to play in deciding the duration of a prisoner's confinement after the judge imposed the sentence.

The states are different. Once a state judge renders a sentence, the judge is usually out of the picture, and parole is the order of the day. On February 26, 2019, the Prison Policy Initiative released a report analyzing the parole release systems of all fifty states and graded them. Its analysis was predicated on statistics and information garnered by the Robina Institute of Criminal Law and Criminal Justice at the University of Minnesota, and the grading was the handiwork of Jorge Renaud, a Prison Policy Initiative senior policy analyst.

As the report first comments,

> [s]ixteen states have abolished or severely curtailed discretionary parole, and the remaining states range from having a system of presumptive parole—where when certain conditions are met, release on parole is guaranteed—to having policies and practices that make earning release almost impossible.

Incredibly, only one state received as high as a B rating, five states got Cs, eight states got Ds, and the remaining thirty-six got an F or F-.[15]

This book is divided into four parts. The first part tells the stories of six representative federal prisoners who had asked me to let them out of jail. Some were serving life sentences for murder. You will learn all about them and the heinous crimes they committed. And at the end of each story, you will wonder what I did.

The second part will tell you about the controversial First Step Act and how it has changed the federal sentencing landscape in the United States.

The third part will tell you what I did with respect to the six prisoners you read about in the first part: Did I let their original sentences stand, or did I give them a second chance? You will be the judge. But try your best to resist the temptation to go directly from the first part to the third part so that you will understand the First Step Act and why I let some murderers out of jail—and not others.

In the fourth part I explain why the states' parole systems have failed us and why the Prison Policy Initiative gave all but one state horrible grades. It will serve as my clarion call to all the states to follow Congress's lead and enact their own First Step acts. I will also explain the devastating effect that thousands of irrational and unnecessary state and federal collateral consequences have on those released from jail after having served their time, and why most consequences should be eliminated.

Surely, it is difficult to have much compassion for my representative criminals, especially the mafiosi. But these cases represent the nature of most of the federal compassionate release cases I've had to decide since the First Step Act took effect in 2018. While federal courts, like state courts, handle many less serious crimes, these are typically low-level drug courier cases. Because the sentences for these are usually in the two-to-three-year range, they realistically are not the subject of compassionate release motions. The typical compassionate release motion entails more serious crimes, which carry far longer jail sentences.

In addition to making for captivating reading, the Mafia compassionate release stories I tell in this book serve as a template for adjudicating the range of resentencing cases under the First Step Act. They should also have equal cogency for the states that hopefully will follow Congress's lead.

An epilogue pulls it all together.

PART I
THE CRIMES

1

JUSTIN VOLPE

Justin Volpe was a New York City police officer with an unblemished record. Yet in 1999 he admitted to shoving the broken handle of a broomstick up the rectum of an innocent Black man, Abner Louima.

The case became a national outrage, triggering mass national demonstrations and initiating a rallying cry for police reform. Echoing the national outrage, my late great colleague Judge Eugene Nickerson sentenced Volpe to thirty years after Volpe pled guilty to committing this heinous crime. Never had such a huge sentence been rendered against a police officer for his on-duty conduct.

Because of the unprecedented nature of Volpe's criminal acts and the long sentence meted out to a police officer, Judge Nickerson wrote a lengthy opinion explaining why he decided to put Volpe behind bars for three decades.[1] He believed that the record before him—including an extensive presentence report from the Probation Department—was "more than adequate to support" his factual findings.

Judge Nickerson recounted the events. In the middle of the night of August 9, 1997, several New York City police officers, including Volpe, attempted to disperse a large crowd that had gathered outside a nightclub at Flatbush Avenue in Brooklyn. The crowd had become unruly, and Volpe struggled with an intoxicated patron, who turned out to be a New York City corrections officer, and pushed him to the ground.

Abner Louima came to the inebriated correction officer's aid, but Volpe "attempted to push Louima away from the club." Louima was then twenty-nine years old. He had immigrated to the United States from Haiti in 1991 and become a citizen six years later.

Louima "refused to move and the confrontation escalated." Several police officers approached and tried to handcuff him. At that time, Volpe "was struck hard on the side of his head and knocked to the ground." Volpe thought Louima had hit him, but Louima's cousin, Jay Nicholas, was the culprit and had fled after he struck Volpe. The officers, including Volpe, chased the cousin; Volpe believed he was chasing Louima.

During the chase, Volpe encountered a totally innocent man, Patrick Antoine, "who had not been at the club and was simply on his way home." Volpe yelled at him "and began beating him," striking his head and face with a flashlight. The man "suffered bruises and contusions on his head and a laceration over his right eye that required seven stiches." To add salt to the wound, the totally innocent man was then placed under arrest after several other officers arrived.

Later that morning, Volpe lied to an assistant district attorney about the Antoine incident. Volpe told the ADA that while he was attempting to place Louima in handcuffs, "Antoine pushed and punched him and refused to be handcuffed." Volpe later falsely swore out a complaint charging Antoine with felony assault and other crimes.

Louima had been arrested by other officers while Volpe was chasing Louima's cousin. As those officers were driving Louima to the Seventieth Precinct in their patrol car, they listened to a radio broadcast describing the assailant. The person being described was Louima's cousin, but there was a family resemblance, and the officers mistakenly believed it was Louima. They began beating Louima's body and head, "at least once with an unidentified hard object, inflicting contusions and bruises."

They then radioed that they had Louima in custody. Volpe heard the report and met the arresting officers on their way to the precinct. Volpe then approached Louima, who was in handcuffs in the back of the patrol car, "and beat him on his head and face with a closed fist and a radio." Louima sustained facial lacerations causing "swelling in his mouth and around his eye."

The arresting officers then drove Louima to the precinct. Volpe arrived shortly thereafter. Louima was still in handcuffs, and while he was being processed "his pants and underwear fell to his ankles."

What happened thereafter haunts me to this day.

Volpe saw Louima at the front desk. He then walked to a room "where he grabbed a wooden broom stick and broke it over his knees." Louima had in the meantime been taken to the bathroom by the two drivers of the car. He was still in handcuffs and his pants and underwear were still around his ankles. Volpe followed him.

Volpe then took out the stick and told Louima: "I'm going to do something to you. If you yell or make any noise, I'll kill you." He then pushed Louima to the ground, with his head near a toilet bowl, and "forced the broken broomstick approximately six inches into Louima's rectum." With Louima "crying and in severe pain," Volpe lifted him and put him in a holding cell.

A few hours later, Louima and Antoine were taken to the hospital. There, Antoine was stitched up to close his lacerations and was released. But doctors had to surgically repair a two-centimeter perforation to Louima's rectum and a three-centimeter perforation to his bladder, as well as perform colostomy and cystostomy procedures.

Louima remained hospitalized for the next two months. He suffered further intestinal complications requiring emergency surgery and the implantation of a colostomy bag. The bag was removed four months later. He thereafter received medical and psychiatric treatment on an outpatient basis "and continued to suffer severe headaches, abdominal pain and insomnia."

When then mayor Rudy Giuliani was first told of the attack by Charles Campisi, the head of the NYPD's Internal Affairs Bureau, before the news hit the media, the mayor exclaimed, "Oh my God. I can't imagine what that man has gone through." Four days later, in his Pulitzer Prize–winning report, *Daily News* columnist Mike McAlary wrote, "This is a tale straight from the police dungeon, an allegation of brutality at the hands of cops from Brooklyn's 70th Precinct that seems so impossible, so crudely medieval." He quoted Louima as saying from his hospital bed: "[The officers] said, 'Take this, nigger,' and stuck the stick in. . . ."[2]

The Louima affair provoked national outrage. Ten days after the attack, an estimated seven thousand demonstrators marched to city hall in protest and shut down the Brooklyn Bridge and parts of Broadway in Lower Manhattan. The march was dubbed "Day of Outrage Against Police Brutality and Harassment." A Black New Jersey police officer captured the sentiment of the marchers, telling CNN: "We're here to send a message to America that people of color will not sit idly by when someone is brutalized."[3]

Volpe was arrested and charged with a host of violent federal crimes. He chose to go to trial, but three days before the scheduled close of oral arguments, after more than two weeks of trial testimony and evidence had been presented to a jury, he agreed to plead guilty to the following counts, rather than risk hearing a devastating jury verdict: (1) conspiring to deprive Louima of his civil rights by aggravated assault and aggravated sexual abuse, (2) assaulting Louima in a police car, (3) sexually abusing Louima in the bathroom of the Seventieth Precinct, (4) assaulting Patrick Antoine, (5) falsely arresting Antoine, and (6) witness tampering. He presumably thought that throwing himself at the mercy of the court would enhance his chances of avoiding a life sentence.

In 1984, Congress created a sentencing commission and charged it with creating guidelines for each crime. Each crime carried a certain number of points. For example, the base level for Extortion Extension of Credit was twenty points. Certain enhancements could increase the number, such as if the extortion involved brandishing a gun or if the defendant had acted in a supervisory role. There could also be an offset if the defendant had accepted responsibility instead of going to trial and either pled guilty to the entire indictment or entered into a plea agreement with the government. The base level for being a participant in a first-degree murder was forty-three points. Pursuant to these guidelines, the Probation Department calculated Volpe's total offense level to be forty-six points.

The guidelines also considered the defendant's criminal history, ranging from a level I to a level VI. If the defendant had committed a lot of other crimes, he or she could hit the jackpot at the highest level. A grid would then instruct the sentencing judge of a sentencing range. For example, seventeen points with a criminal history of level III would carry a range of thirty to thirty-seven months. The judge would then have discretion to fix a sentence within that range, after considering the nature of the crime against the defendant's personal characteristics. There were also some limited possibilities of going below the range if, by way of one example, the defendant suffered from extreme mental illness. And the judge could even impose a sentence above the range if the highest criminal history category underrepresented a very bad apple.

As for Volpe, since the minimum level for life imprisonment was forty-three points, the Probation Department recommended that a life sentence must be imposed. Judge Nickerson, however, disagreed with that guidelines calculation. He determined that the proper level was forty-two points and imposed a sentence of 360 months. Finally, the judge ordered restitution for Louima of $277,495.09.

In his opinion, Judge Nickerson commented on the "unique depravity" of Volpe's heinous crime: "Short of intentional murder, one cannot imagine a more barbarous misuse of power." Nonetheless, because of Volpe's status as a police officer, which, when combined with the case's extended national publicity, exposed Volpe to abuse by other prisoners or segregation, Judge Nickerson cut him a break and thought three decades of imprisonment were sufficient.

Judge Nickerson did not have a reputation as a harsh sentencer, and Volpe's gamble to plead guilty to avoid a life sentence paid off. Judge Nickerson acknowledged, however, that "[i]t would be difficult indeed to 'overstate the harm' Volpe inflicted upon Louima and upon society at large." Thus, the judge rejected a host of other arguments that Volpe made for more downward adjustments, concluding that Volpe's sexual assault against Louima was "extraordinary" because of "its violence and its commission by a uniformed police officer against a handcuffed prisoner."

Before Judge Nickerson imposed his sentence, he listened to Volpe speak in a packed courtroom—as was Volpe's right. He tearfully pleaded for mercy, apologized to his two victims, and admitted that he indeed jammed a broken broomstick into Louima's rectum, inflicting severe internal injuries, because he mistakenly believed that Louima had punched him in the head during a street brawl.

He told Judge Nickerson that he "was ashamed and deeply regretful for what [he] did" and added: "I betrayed Abner Louima's rights, I betrayed the city's confidence in police officers, I betrayed myself and my partners and I betrayed my lawyer." This last reference was because he had not told his lawyer that he was guilty until the trial evidence was overwhelming. What was missing, however, was an acknowledgment by Volpe that even if Louima were guilty of striking him, it would not have justified Volpe's actions at the police station.

Volpe's sentence drew sharply mixed reactions. Federal prosecutors said they accepted it, although they had urged Judge Nickerson to impose a life term. Not surprisingly, Volpe's lawyer and father both called it too harsh, while Louima's supporters insisted it was too lenient. Calling the sentence appropriate, Police Commissioner Howard Safir said, "I hope this is a chapter in the history of the N.Y.P.D. that is behind us."[4] The double entendre was presumably unintended.

In an extensive opinion, the court of appeals unanimously affirmed Judge Nickerson's sentence, concluding that "the district judge did not err."[5]

Not surprisingly, the Volpe case attracted a lot of post-conviction media attention. Volpe's mother was quick to point out that one of the most troubling aspects of her son's thirty-year sentence was that it came on the same day a cop killer was sentenced to possible less time. Indeed, Shatiek Johnson, eighteen, who was convicted of the 1999 murder of housing police officer Gerard Carter—known as "the gentle giant"—received a minimum sentence that was five years less than Volpe's. Volpe's mother told the *New York Post* that Johnson "killed someone and had a previous homicide and other acts of violence, and my son didn't kill anyone."[6]

But in general, the public was puzzled as to how Volpe could do such a horrific thing to another human being. And the psychological pundits had a field day. They pondered whether Volpe could have been the product of a bad neighborhood or a dysfunctional family. But his mother was an artist, as was his father, who became a cop. Volpe grew up comfortably in a middle-class neighborhood on Staten Island, attended a Catholic high school, and graduated from St. John's University.

None of Volpe's fellow police officers described the handsome, white, twenty-seven-year-old Volpe as an outsider, a reject, a nerd, or any of the things that might drive people to commit hateful crimes. More surprisingly, given the racist language he had used in assaulting Louima, for several years Volpe dated and became engaged to a Black female clerk at his precinct. He ultimately married a white woman in 2012, in a ceremony where he was housed at the low-security Coleman Florida Federal Correctional Facility.

Volpe had been on the force for four years before his inexplicable crime, had received merit badges for excellent police work, and had never been disciplined for police misconduct. His conduct in brutalizing Louima was aberrational and why he did that remains a psychological mystery to this day.

As for Abner Louima, he sat silently during the sentencing, but he subsequently brought a civil lawsuit against New York City. In 2001, in the largest New York City settlement for police brutality at the time, the city and the police union agreed to pay Louima a total of $8.75 million, of which Louima collected $5.8 million, the rest paid out to Louima's lawyers.[7] Using the settlement money, Louima set up a nonprofit group, the Abner Louima Foundation, dedicated to building community centers in Haiti and for Haitians in the United States, and paid the school tuition for fourteen low-income children from the town in Haiti where he grew up. In a 2003 interview, Louima said, "Maybe God saved my life for a reason. I believe in doing the right thing."[8]

On August 9, 2007, the tenth anniversary of the attack, the National Action Network held an event honoring Louima and reflecting on the legacy of Volpe's attack. Louima was then running a successful real estate business and living quietly in Florida with his wife and children. On that occasion, he wrote an editorial in the *New York Daily News*, commenting, "Things may have improved a bit, but not enough."[9]

Years later, he told the *New York Post* that as a Christian he has forgiven Volpe "but will never forget." However, he added, "My life has changed in the worst imaginable way" and that he still suffers emotionally. He explained, "I will live with the pain for the rest of my life. I will suffer for the rest of my life. When something that bad happens to you, it's something you have to live with and feel every day." He deals with it by "pretend[ing] that it wasn't real."

As for his feelings about Volpe, he told the newspaper, "I'm sure he's paid for what he's done. He knows what he did, and if he wants to repent, it will be up to him."[10]

Notably, Volpe had ended his remarks before Judge Nickerson sentenced him by telling the judge that he had "come to realize that this case goes beyond [him] and Abner Louima."

He could not have been more prescient. Although the Louima attack was certainly not the first case of police brutality in our nation's history, its stark inhumanity and revulsive nature against an innocent Black man sparked heightened national efforts to address police brutality and contributed to the emergence of the Black Lives Matter movement. Analysts have identified myriad causes of police violence, including the predominantly white and male composition of the police force, historic racism and racial stereotyping, a "siege mentality" among officers, and a culture of impunity.[11]

Since the Louima nightmare, many cities have implemented

concerted efforts to address those concerns, but whether they have gone far enough and have been successful remains the subject of intense debate.

Unfortunately, the Louima case has subsequently been trumped by other recent notorious displays of police brutality, most notably the George Floyd chokehold case, which also provoked national outrage. But Louima's was the first case in New York City (and perhaps elsewhere) in which a police officer was tried and convicted for police brutality. It stands out to the present for its historical significance in our nation's efforts to address and remedy the root causes of police brutality.

On December 10, 2020, Volpe brought a compassionate release motion before me under the First Step Act. He was then almost forty-eight years old and had served twenty-one and a half years of his thirty-year sentence, and he asked me to set him free.

2

SHERWIN BIRKETT

Sherwin Birkett was arrested on November 30, 1990, when he was not quite twenty. After a jury trial the next summer, he was found guilty of charges under the Racketeer Influenced and Corrupt Organizations Act (RICO) dating back to when he was nine years old—"that from 1979 until December 6, 1990," he and others "were associated with the Vassell Enterprise and participated in a pattern of racketeering activity involving a 'Conspiracy to Possess and Distribute Substantial Quantities of Heroin, Cocaine and Cocaine Base.'"

RICO was enacted by Congress in 1970 specifically to fight organized crime. Under RICO, "it is a crime for an individual to belong to an 'enterprise' that is involved in a pattern of racketeering activity, even if that criminal activity was committed by other people."[1] As two scholars explain,

> The power of RICO lies in its conspiracy provision, based on an enterprise rationale, that allows tying

together apparently unrelated crimes with a common
objective into a prosecutable pattern of racketeering.
In addition, RICO provides for severer penalties and
permits a defendant to be convicted and separately punished for both the underlying crimes that constitute the
pattern of racketeering activity and for a substantive
violation of RICO.[2]

Birkett was also charged and found guilty, together with codefendant Paul A. Moore, of aiding and abetting "the murder of Harry Emanuel Spence ('Jamaican Bob') while engaged in racketeering
activity."

The trial judge, my colleague Reena Raggi, sentenced Birkett to
life on December 20, 1992. I was not on the court at that time. Under
the then mandatory guidelines, she had no choice. But she had been
given an elaborate presentence report by the Probation Department
explaining the vast Vassell criminal enterprise and Birkett's role
in it. I read it carefully when I had to decide—twenty-one years
later—whether to grant Birkett's compassionate release motion.

Birkett was one of forty-seven codefendants who were indicted
in this vast RICO conspiracy because of an extensive investigation that began in late March 1990 "when agents of the Bureau of
Alcohol, Tobacco and Firearms and the Federal Bureau of Investigation teamed up with the New York City Police to investigate a
violent narcotics conspiracy, run by Jamaican nationals, operating
in the Crown Heights neighborhood of Brooklyn." It began when
a conspirator, fearing for his life, voluntarily went to Brooklyn's
Seventy-Seventh Police Precinct and gave detailed information
that "would lead to the uncovering of a multi-million-dollar drug
operation that had been prospering, growing, and branching out
for over a decade."

Ultimately, the investigators learned that over fifty participants were involved in a hierarchy headed by a single kingpin, Eric Vassell. When he was twenty, Vassell fled Jamaica and arrived illegally in the United States, where he set up a marijuana distribution "spot" on Kosciuszko Street in Brooklyn. Soon, Vassell became the leader of a handful of other Jamaicans, selling $10 bags of cocaine from a "social club" on Schenectady Avenue in Crown Heights.

Vassell proved to be quite the entrepreneur. He assembled a "posse" of criminals to do his bidding, and by 1983, when he was just twenty-four years old, was generating $5,000 per day in cocaine sales and another $5,000 per day in heroin sales. By 1987, his posse was generating $50,000 weekly in cocaine sales and $70,000 in weekly heroin sales. Vassell was becoming so wealthy that during that year he purchased a large fifty-nine-unit apartment building in Crown Heights with his narcotics proceeds.

Ultimately, Vassell resorted to murdering "outsiders" to expand his enterprise, which had thrived for almost a decade, until December 1990. During that time, he had branched out to Dallas, Texas, where he established a multi-kilo crack cocaine distribution network.

Over time, the government's investigation linked numerous arrests to Vassell's posse, "including incidents at the Canadian border, a federal firearms prosecution in Florida, fraudulent document investigations, narcotics arrests, currency seizures, drug seizures, firearms arrests and the discovery of several dead, bullet-ridden bodies in Dallas and New York."

The Vassell Enterprise came tumbling down when on December 6, 1990, search and arrest warrants were simultaneously executed by a massive number of law enforcement personnel—estimated to be approximately four hundred—in Brooklyn, Dallas, Albany (where a crack distribution manager had relocated), and Long Island (where homes were owned by posse members). Seized during the raids were large retail and wholesale quantities of marijuana, cocaine, and heroin, as well as lots of drug paraphernalia, dozens of loaded guns, bulletproof vests, over $100,000 in cash, and "thousands of dollars worth of gold and diamond jewelry."

As the indictment read, the sale of retail quantities of narcotics "was the sole reason for the existence of the posse" and "ancillary activities—from murders to the purchasing of properties, from attaining fraudulent passports to money laundering"—were all acts to further the enterprise's retail distribution business.

And Eric Vassell participated in or ordered plenty of murders and attempted murders, particularly over the span of several months in 1988 and 1989. These ranged the scope of Vassell's violent, demented mentality. For example, on July 9, 1988, Cedrick Miller was shot once in the head and once in the neck because he belonged to a rival Jamaican political party. Then, in October of 1989, posse member Everton Henry was purposely shot in the leg because he had shown disrespect to Vassell while inside Vassell's social club. On February 13, 1989, Arnold Blake was kidnapped at gunpoint, had his dreadlocks forcibly cut off, and was severely beaten by Vassell and others for not responding when called by Vassell. Lawrence Southerland was murdered at Vassell's behest in 1988 because he was known to have sold crack on posse territory. Also in 1988, posse member Kirk Boreland was shot to death upon orders from Vassell because he had been high on crack and was disrupting the posse's narcotics distribution business.

The day after Christmas in 1989, Devon Grant, known to have participated in posse murders, was shot to death because he was "annoying" Vassell and was accused of robbing the home of a posse member. The next May, posse member Anthony Goffe was murdered on orders of Vassell because Goffe was spending time with Fitzgerald Reid, a former posse member, while Vassell was feuding with Reid's brother; several days later, Reid was shot to death.

In earlier years, Colin Goodridge was beaten and shot to death by Vassell and others because he was suspected of being an informant for the Jamaican police. Joscelyn Dudley Watson, the owner and landlord of a neighborhood building, was shot to death under Vassell's orders because Watson would often call police to the neighborhood. Vassell subsequently bought the building.

Sherwin Birkett was implicated in the murder of Harold Spence on April 7, 1989, which formed the basis of his RICO charge. Spence was murdered in an alley in Dallas. He was found lying faceup against a hog wire fence with a loaded .44 caliber pistol in his hand. He had been shot multiple times in the face, chest, back, stomach, and arms by Birkett and his codefendant, Paul Moore. Spence was a rival Jamaican crack dealer in Dallas who had disrespected members of the Vassell organization earlier that day.

In the presentence report, Birkett was described by agents as "an enforcer employed with the Vassell Organization, primarily in their Dallas crack distribution network since 1988." He was then only eighteen years old. Birkett was frequently observed by agents at the crack distribution location in Dallas used by the Vassell organization. It was estimated that the organization distributed approximately 28.5 kilograms of crack during 1988, 1989, and 1990. The agents portrayed Birkett "as at times, acting in a supervisory capacity since he occasionally directed other workers and assured they were fully supplied with crack."

Birkett was born in Barbados on December 24, 1970, and was reared by his mother, maternal grandmother, and an aunt. He had had no contact with his father since he was one year old. He came to the United States with his mother when he was ten. She became employed as a home attendant for elderly people. When Birkett was sixteen years old, he moved from his mother's home to Dallas, where he lived until his arrest. During his presentence interview, when asked why he went there, he simply stated that he "went there with several other guys to work a spot."

* * *

As I was reading the presentence report I wondered why the Vassell Enterprise was able to make so much money in the United States selling drugs. I remembered when I was on an airplane a few years ago, flying to Tampa from New York to visit my brother. Sitting next to me was an interesting and bright woman. She was a psychologist and we struck up a conversation. When she told me that she was born in Medellín, Colombia, I told her that I had recently sentenced a Medellín drug kingpin to twenty years in prison and asked her why we had such a huge drug problem in the United States. She reminded me of Adam Smith's classic 1776 book *The Wealth of Nations*, about the law of supply and demand. "My dear Judge Block," she began, "if there were no demand for drugs in the United States, there would be no supply." Her logic was impeccable, and when I returned to my chambers, I did a little "drug research."

The history of drug use in our country and Congress's reactions trace its beginnings to the racism and xenophobia that motivated early drug laws. Many kinds of intoxicants were available in the mid- to late nineteenth century and the early part of the twentieth century; nevertheless, only those drugs that were associated with nonwhite racial groups were targeted.

The first antidrug law was a local law passed in San Francisco in 1875. It outlawed the smoking of opium and was directed at the Chinese because opium smoking was a peculiarly Chinese habit. It was believed that Chinese men were luring white women to have sex in opium dens. In 1909, Congress made opium smoking a federal offense by enacting the Anti-Opium Act. It reinforced Chinese racism by carving out an exception for drinking and injecting tinctures of opiates that were popular among white people.

Cocaine regulations also were triggered by racial prejudice. Cocaine use was associated with Black people, just as opium use was associated with Chinese people. Newspaper articles bore racially charged headlines linking cocaine with violent, antisocial behavior by Black people. A 1914 *New York Times* article proclaimed: "Negro Cocaine 'Fiends' Are a New Southern Menace: Murder and Insanity Increasing Among Lower Class Blacks Because They Have Taken to 'Sniffing.'" A *Literary Digest* article from the same year claimed that "most of the attacks upon women in the South are the direct result of the cocaine-crazed Negro brain."

It came as no surprise, therefore, that 1914 was also the year that Congress passed the Harrison Narcotics Tax Act, effectively outlawing opium and cocaine.

Marijuana prohibition also had racist underpinnings. This time it was the Mexicans. Just as cocaine was associated with Black violence and irrational behavior, in the southwestern border towns marijuana was viewed—beginning in the early 1920s—as a cause of Mexican lawlessness. A Texas police captain suggested that marijuana gave Mexicans superhuman strength to commit acts of violence:

> Under marijuana Mexicans [become] very violent, especially when they become angry and will attack an officer even if a gun is drawn on him. They seem to have no fear. I have also noted that under the influence of this weed they have enormous strength and it will take several men to handle one man while, under ordinary circumstances, one man could handle him with ease.

The American Coalition—an anti-immigrant group—claimed as recently as 1980 that "[m]arijuana, perhaps now the most insidious of narcotics, is a direct by-product of unrestricted Mexican immigration."[3]

The racial fallout from our drug laws has persevered. In her article appearing in the *Alabama Law Review*, "The Discrimination

Inherent in America's Drug War," Kathleen R. Sandy reported in 2003 that Black Americans then constituted approximately 12% of our country's population and 13% of drug users. Nevertheless, they accounted for 33% of all drug-related arrests, 62% of drug-related convictions, and 70% of drug-related incarcerations.[4]

The country's concerted crackdown on drugs—and the imposition of increasingly harsh punishment for illicit usage, importation, and distribution—probably owes its genesis to the appointment by the head of the Treasury Department in 1930 of Harry Anslinger as the commissioner of the newly created Federal Bureau of Narcotics. Anslinger started a media campaign to classify marijuana as a dangerous drug, publishing a major article in the *American Magazine* titled "Marijuana: The Assassin of Youth." It was rife with accusations that marijuana was responsible for encouraging murder, suicide, and insanity. Anslinger's campaign was wildly successful. Before he took office, only four states had enacted prohibitions against nonmedical usage of marijuana—California (1915), Texas (1919), Louisiana (1924), and New York (1927)—but by 1937, forty-six of the nation's then forty-eight states had banned marijuana.

Since then, Congress has enacted a spate of comprehensive antidrug laws with strict penalties. For example, one could be sentenced to life for distributing 1 kilogram of heroin; forty years for distributing 100 grams, and twenty years for distributing any quantity at all. Nonetheless, this did not stem the country's appetite for illicit drugs in spite of every administration's continued "war on drugs" since President Nixon established the Drug Enforcement Administration in 1972. By 2012, the DEA had grown to a staff of almost ten thousand employees and a budget of $2 billion.[5]

According to data from the 2023 National Survey on Drug Use and Health, over 143 million Americans aged twelve or older—50.7% of that population at that time—reported illicit drug use at least once in their lives; 24.9% admitted to using an illegal drug in the prior year; and 16.5% (roughly 46 million people) did it within the prior month.[6] The National Center for Drug Abuse Statistics reported that 1 out of every 16 high school seniors smoked marijuana on a daily basis in 2023.[7]

It was no wonder, therefore, that Vassell's drug distribution business was booming.

Heroin and cocaine are still deadly drugs today. But they have now been surpassed by more deadly ones. Unsuspecting users of fentanyl are now dying every day. I have sentenced ignorant, low-level distributors of that drug—who were not remotely aware of its deadly impact—to long prison terms.

But the world has changed with respect to marijuana. Presently, twenty-four states and the District of Columbia have legalized it for adult recreational use.[8] Nevertheless, because of our system of federalism, although the states can authorize the sale and distribution of homegrown marijuana, these are still federal crimes. Thus, marijuana remains classified as a Schedule I drug under federal law, meaning that it is viewed by the federal government as one of the most serious and deadly drugs.

The upshot is that although possessing and smoking marijuana may not be a state crime in those states that have legalized it, a person can still be prosecuted under federal law. It is a tortuous conflict.

The area of law that addresses possible conflicts between state and federal law is generally referred to as the Supremacy Clause of the U.S. Constitution. Within that clause is the doctrine of preemption, which dictates that in many (but not all) cases of conflicting laws, federal law supersedes state law. The Supreme Court may someday have to decide if the federal marijuana laws preempt the state marijuana laws. In the meantime, we have an awkward stalemate: in the states that have legalized marijuana, the federal government has not tried to push back through enforcement or preemption actions. This undoubtedly reflects a changing attitude about smoking pot, much like the evolution in the public's opposition to the prohibition of alcohol a hundred years ago.

I got Birkett's case when it was reassigned to me after my colleague Sterling Johnson passed away in December 2022. Judge Johnson was a revered judge. He rose from walking the beat in Harlem as a policeman to distinguishing himself for thirty-one years as a jurist. Among his celebrated cases was his ordering the closing of a Guantánamo Bay detention facility, which he deemed an "H.I.V. prison camp" for Haitian refugees. He later ruled that New York City had failed to assist poor residents with AIDS adequately. He was the special narcotics prosecutor for New York City in 1991 when President George H.W. Bush nominated him for the district bench.

For all his wonderful attributes, Judge Johnson was hardly a good draw for Birkett. He supported harsh sentences for drug dealers and had a reputation for being tough on Black defendants. He would often tell them when he imposed a high sentence that if he could make it as a Black man, there was no excuse for them to resort to crime. He was proud of his accomplishments and embarrassed by their misdeeds.

In 2009, Judge Johnson denied Birkett's motion to have his life sentence changed. Birkett had argued that the law had changed since he was sentenced in 1992 in several respects. Judge Johnson disagreed. Although the First Step Act had yet to be enacted in 1992, Judge Johnson wrote that even if he had the power to do so, he would not change the sentence because of "the serious and violent nature of the offense (murder), as well as Birkett's history of disciplinary violations while in custody."[9]

Birkett languished in prison for the next thirteen years, when in 2022, in response to a compassionate release request from his codefendant, Paul Moore, I reduced Moore's life sentence to thirty-five years, meaning Moore would soon be released from prison in his late fifties.[10]

Moore had come to the United States from Jamaica, and when he was a teenager he also came under Eric Vassell's spell. In his early twenties, Moore was directed by Vassell to "expand . . . operations of the violent drug ring to Texas." The joint murder of Harold Spence by Birkett and Moore served as Moore's predicate RICO murder count.

When Judge Raggi sentenced Moore to life, she commented: "[The] argument that the defendant should be given some hope is not without considerable appeal to the Court, but I do not see a principled ground for departure and I am obliged to follow the guidelines."

But in his request to me for compassionate release, Moore was represented by excellent counsel. Moore's attorney correctly stated that Judge Raggi's sentence "was dictated by a sentencing regime that was declared unconstitutional in [United States v.] Booker," when in 2005, the Supreme Court held that the federal sentencing guidelines were discretionary and no longer mandatory. As Moore's attorney further stated, his client "had satisfied the First Step Act's first prong that this constituted 'an extraordinary and compelling factor.'"

I made the decision to release Moore, convinced in part by the attorney's argument, as I stated in my opinion, that of all of those indicted under the RICO charge, "[o]nly Moore and one of his 46 co-defendants [were] serving life sentences." That other person was, of course, Sherwin Birkett. All the others were serving sentences of thirty-three years or less.

Shockingly, Eric Vassell, the brutal killer and leader of the Vassell

Enterprise, must have had a great lawyer. Obviously, if Vassell went to trial, he would have been convicted for many brutal murders as the leader of the Vassell Enterprise and would justifiably have been sentenced to die in prison. But his skilled lawyer negotiated a plea deal that would release his notorious client from prison in December 2022, after having served twenty-five years. This inexplicable sentencing disparity was the main reason I let Moore out of prison.

But what about Birkett? He had filed a motion for compassionate release, and because he was indigent he had asked for a lawyer. It was in my discretion to assign one, but it would cost a lot of taxpayer monies if everyone who filed a compassionate release motion were given a lawyer. I wondered what I should do.

3

JOE SMITH

On July 9, 2018, Joe Smith pled guilty to the receipt of child porn. I refer to him as "Joe Smith" throughout to protect his anonymity because of the sensitive nature of his crime.

Child pornography prosecutions in the Eastern District of New York have proliferated from the beginning of the internet; I call them internet crimes. I've had my share and have put otherwise law-abiding citizens—many of them prominent members of their communities—in jail for long stretches. These people were not "criminals" in the common understanding of that word. But they all shared one thing in common: a perverted need to watch or distribute salacious videos or photos of minors, and to engage minors in provocative sexual internet chatter. Some even went so far as to try to arrange to meet children for illicit, depraved sexual conduct.

Not surprisingly, Congress took swift and punitive action. It established high mandatory minimums for many child pornography crimes. Thus, the receipt of child porn called for a five-year mandatory sentence. If you were guilty of producing or trafficking in child pornography, the mandatory minimum was fifteen years.

In statistics compiled by the Sentencing Commission for fiscal year 2020, 1,023 people had been convicted that year of child pornography. Of the people convicted, 45.1% were sentenced for possession, 41.9% were sentenced for production or trafficking, and 13% were sentenced for receiving child pornography. And of that number, 99.7% were men; 81.3% were white, 12.2% were Hispanic, and 4% were Black. Their average age was forty-two years, and 96.8% were U.S. citizens. Of the offenders, 90.5% were convicted of an offense carrying a five-year mandatory minimum.[1]

Congress's high minimum jail terms were politically popular with an understandably emotional public, outraged that anyone would prey on children. My own adult daughters, Tina and Debbie, were no exceptions. If it were up to them, anyone producing or even viewing them "should all be shot or put in jail for life."

But such is not the law; nor should it be. Society needs to be protected from people with these proclivities, but we cannot simply warehouse them in prison. Among other reasons, being exposed to violent criminals makes them easy prey for physical abuse. My own opinion is that they need to be housed in a facility that can professionally address and hopefully abate their addiction and then be subject to lifetime supervision. However, Congress has decided to criminalize their behavior and to incarcerate them with the general prison population.

Joe Smith was born abroad in 1976, but he and his parents came to the United States when he was just two years old, and they all ultimately became U.S. citizens. Smith lived with his wife and two young children in a small, well-furnished apartment in an upscale neighborhood. At the time he was arrested in 2015, his children— both boys—were four years and eighteen months old. He was well educated and was earning $160,000 annually as a computer pro-grammer and systems integrator at a major bank.

Smith's problems began when the FBI investigated a web-site ("Website A") that operated on an alternative network (the "Network") available to internet users who were aware of its exis-tence. The Network was designed to facilitate anonymous commu-nication over the internet. Websites that were accessible only to users within the Network could be set up within the Network, and Website A was one such website. Thus, Website A could not gener-ally be accessed through the traditional internet. Only a user who had installed the appropriate software on the user's computer could access it. Smith was one such user.

Website A was a child pornography bulletin board and website dedicated to the advertisement and distribution of child pornogra-phy and the discussion of matters pertinent to the sexual abuse of children, including the safety and security of individuals who seek to sexually exploit children online in a secret manner. In 2015, the computer server hosting Website A was seized from a web-hosting facility. During the ensuing weeks, law enforcement agents acting pursuant to a court order from another federal district court moni-tored electronic communications of users of Website A.

According to data from logs on Website A, an individual who would later be identified as Smith had registered an account on that website under a fictitious name. Under that name, Smith accessed numerous posts containing sexually explicit images, including prepubescent females. For example, he accessed the post entitled "Seagirl and Sister (700 unsorted images)." This post contained hundreds of child pornography thumbnail images of young females ranging in age from about four to ten years old engaging in various sexual activities with adult men, as well as with themselves.

Smith had also accessed a post that contained a link to thirty-four images. One image depicted a little girl who looked like she was about five years old. She appeared to be passed out while an adult male penetrated her vagina with his penis.

It was a simple thing for the FBI to then obtain a warrant to search Smith's home and his computer. He was present when the agents arrived. They recovered a memory card, cellular phone, and a network-attached storage device that was an external hard drive that connects to the internet instead of to a computer. The FBI agents performed a preliminary review of these devices and discovered that they contained approximately thirty thousand computer files of child pornography images and videos.

Among the files that the agents viewed was a video depicting a nude prepubescent girl being anally penetrated by what appeared to be an adult male penis. The agents also viewed a video file depicting a nude prepubescent girl, who appeared to be between six and seven, touching her vagina in a bathtub and performing oral sex on an adult male.

Smith was then arrested. He fully cooperated with the agents and, after being read his rights, volunteered detailed accounts of his aberrant sexual behavior. He admitted that he began viewing child pornography after learning about the Network on a documentary. This led him to a child pornography website. He also learned that he could launch the Network from a CD, rather than from a desktop, thereby limiting his criminal exposure and the likelihood that he would be caught.

Smith acknowledged that he accessed child pornography from Website A and that he used a fictitious name as his username. The agents showed him some of his files that contained child porn, and he confirmed that he had downloaded them. He told them that he masturbated to those images about once a week when his wife and children were out of the apartment.

In addition to Website A, Smith accessed similar websites on the Network. He described himself as more of a "lurker" but admitted that he also used peer-to-peer programs to download child pornography. He knew that by doing that he was passively sharing the pornography.

Smith admitted that he downloaded hundreds of files of child porn depicting children who appeared to be from six to twelve years old, and that they were mostly little girls. He described himself as a "gatherer" and had "a lot of stuff," including bestiality. However, he denied ever having sexual contact with any minors, including his own children, and agreed to take a polygraph test. He flunked the test but continued to deny that he had ever had sexual contact with a minor.

As mandated reporters, the FBI agents made a report to the New York State Central Registry Office of Child and Family Services. The agency's case agent reviewed all the contents of Smith's electronic devices. The agent informed the FBI that Smith had compiled 56,658 images and 289 videos of child pornography. An effort was made to locate the victims, but none were found.

In 2018, Smith negotiated a plea deal with the government and pled guilty before a magistrate judge to count 1 of a two-count indictment. The count charged him with "receiving and possessing one or more visual depictions," specifically, the post entitled "Seagirl and Sister" and the one with the girl in the bathtub.

I was the judge in Smith's case and had allowed Smith to be out on bail for a little over three years while his lawyer was bringing pretrial motions and desperately, but unsuccessfully, trying to talk the government into a plea deal that would not require the five-year mandatory minimum. During his time at liberty, he was totally compliant with the stringent bail conditions I imposed, including home confinement and no internet access.

I felt sorry for his wife and two children. They were with him the first time he had appeared before me. I recall his wife weeping in the first row. She was holding her eighteen-month-old son on her lap. Her four-year-old son was sitting next to her clinging to her dress. I let her speak to me. She told me her husband was a "wonderful man and great father." He had never laid a hand on the boys. She was not employed and needed him to help take care of the children. She would not know what to do without him. But she had no idea her husband had "this problem."

When I finally had to sentence Smith, his wife and children were there. The baby was now three, and the elder son was seven. I had ordered a forensic evaluation and was pleased to learn that his wife and children were well taken care of and had benefited from his prolonged stay at home.

Before I calculated the guidelines range, I had a spirited discussion with the assistant U.S. attorney. Initially, I was puzzled to understand the difference between possession of child pornography, which did not carry a mandatory minimum, and receipt, which, as in Smith's case, required me to sentence him to a minimum of five years. I asked counsel, "I don't know how you can possess something without receiving it?" I never got a satisfactory answer. The best the government could say was that "theoretically, Your Honor, you could possess an item that you come across and not receive it."

Nonetheless, there was no question in this case that Smith received his child pornography from the internet.

Next, I had to calculate the guideline range. It came out to be between 97 and 121 months, well above the 60-month minimum, and the government asked that I sentence him within that range. But the high range was driven by the fact that the website he accessed contained over fifty thousand images, which required a significant increase in the guideline calculation. In other words, as soon as you accessed the website, you were deemed to have received every image on that website.

However, Smith was charged with having viewed only two of

the images, and it was highly unlikely that he viewed all fifty thousand. This led to a discussion of the recent decision of the Second Circuit Court of Appeals in the *Dorvee* case, where the appellate court cautioned against applying an unrealistic guideline. There, it reversed a guidelines sentence of 240 months and sent the case back to the district court for a more reasonable sentence. The court chastised Congress for providing an unrealistic pornography guideline. It held that the guideline was "fundamentally different" from most other guidelines and must be applied with "great care" because it was not based on the Sentencing Commission's expertise, but rather on Congress's direction. It pointed out that the guideline irrationally recommended a higher sentence than for those given to adults who actually engage in sex with minors.

I sentenced Smith, therefore, to the five-year mandatory minimum. This was also the Probation Department's recommendation. Before I formally imposed the sentence, I invited Smith to speak, which was his right. He was trembling as he rose and read from a printed statement.

> I deeply regret that my actions have harmed others. I will live with this transgression for the rest of my life. With the love and support of my family, I believe I will come out of this experience as a better person.
>
> I'm grateful for the three-and-a-half years that I have been able to be with my family out on bond, but the prospect of my wife having to raise our children alone and the children being raised without a father figure present is hard to accept.
>
> My children are both smart and full of potential. My wife and parents have been so strong through all of this, and they impress me every day. I have tremendous remorse for the pain that I have put them through, but

this is not to dismiss the pain forced onto children in the images that I looked at.

In the course of sex therapy, I have learned what these children and adolescents go through, and that they are not simply objects on the computer screen. I'm filled with remorse and sadness over the harm inflicted on such helpless children and adolescents to get the illegal material I viewed. If for a second I had known what I know now back in 2015, we would not be here right now. I can now say that I will never seek such material again.

I had the opportunity to get the last word:

THE COURT: All right, [Mr. Smith]. It's clear to me that you've accepted responsibility. It's clear to me that you have benefited from all sorts of therapy, and that you are a candidate for resuscitating your life and dealing with these issues, and it seems like you are dealing with them from everything I've read, which is the most important thing, so that in the future, there will not be any future victims, and that's what we really are concerned about.

So the comments I made about my discomfort with mandatory minimums do not mean that I don't find the crime you committed to be distasteful and worthy of punishment. That's a separate standalone concept that I'm troubled with, when I have to have my discretion imposed upon.

But nonetheless, in this situation, it is almost academic because I think 60 months would clearly be indicated, even if there was no mandatory minimum.

As I walked out of the courtroom, I wondered whether, if my daughters were present, they would have thought that Smith should be jailed for life or shot.

It came as no surprise that Smith would bring a compassionate release motion.

4

THE MAFIA CASES: ANTHONY RUSSO

Anthony Russo was born on February 24, 1953. Forty years later he was arrested and charged with seven crimes, two of which were for the murders of John Minerva and Michael Imbergamo "in furtherance of racketeering activity" under RICO. The other charges were for RICO and murder conspiracies, conspiracy to make extortionate extensions of credit, and the use of a firearm during a crime of violence. After a jury trial before my former colleague Judge Charles Sifton, who passed away in 2009, Russo was convicted of all those crimes and sentenced by Judge Sifton in 1994 to life.

One of the most famous RICO cases in the history of the United States, dubbed the "Trial of the Century," was the trial of John Gotti in my Brooklyn courthouse. It is often cited as an example of the successful use of RICO to dismantle organized crime syndicates and prosecute high-profile criminals. The indictment alleged that Gotti engaged in a pattern of illegal activity, including murder, extortion, and money laundering. The prosecution presented evidence of wiretapped conversations and witness testimony to support its case. Although Gotti was twice acquitted of all charges, earning him the appellation of the Teflon Don, he was subsequently convicted in a separate RICO trial and sentenced to life in prison by my colleague Judge I. Leo Glasser. Because there is no age limit for federal judges, Judge Glasser still sits on the bench at the ripe old age of one hundred.

It is reasonable to question whether the Founding Fathers were correct in providing in the Constitution that federal judges may serve for life—barring impeachment for "crimes and misdemeanors." I suspect that it was not a matter of great concern at the time, because people didn't live as long as we do now. But we currently have several federal judges in our country who are still on the bench in their tenth decades, as I am. And Judge Glasser has recently entered his eleventh decade.

All the states have mandatory retirement ages. If I were a state judge in New York, I would have been required to retire when I was seventy—or possibly when I was seventy-six if I passed physical and mental qualification tests. Instead, I am still meting out justice—hopefully—more than twenty years later.

I do not think it would be inappropriate to mandate a retirement age for federal judges. But I'm not sure what that age should be. If the time comes when I do not think I have my "A" game anymore, I will quit. But it's not an easy call. Surely my law clerks are unlikely to tell me when to hang it up, but I will reach out to my colleagues for their input. So far, so good. And the same goes for Judge Glasser, who still is mentally alert and fully functional. Moreover, he is an extraordinary judge and human being, revered by the bench and bar.

My court, the Eastern District of New York, is known as the "Mafia court" because most of the RICO prosecutions of the mafiosi happen there. The district—which covers Brooklyn, Queens, Staten Island, and Nassau and Suffolk Counties—is the proper venue for most of these cases since the defendants often come from Howard Beach in Queens, live in Staten Island, where many of their murdered victims are buried, and hatch their criminal misdeeds at "social clubs" in Brooklyn.

I have had my share of high-profile Mafia cases. Notably, after John Gotti died in jail in 2002 from cancer at the age of sixty-one, he was succeeded as the boss of the Gambino crime family by his son, who was known as Junior. The apple did not fall far from the criminal family tree, and in 1999 Junior pled guilty to racketeering and extortion charges. He was sentenced that year to seventy-seven months in prison. Peter Gotti—the Teflon Don's older brother—then became the acting boss of the Gambino crime family. He had an avuncular demeanor, and the mafiosi called him Uncle Peter.

It didn't take long for the government to indict Peter and sixteen others in a sixty-eight-count indictment. In essence, the government charged the defendants under RICO with being Gambino family members engaged in racketeering schemes victimizing labor unions and businesses operating at piers and terminals in Brooklyn and Staten Island by extortion, illegal gambling, wire fraud, and money laundering.

Nine pled guilty to various crimes. The remaining seven—including Peter—opted to go to trial. But unlike Anthony Russo, Peter was not charged with murders. He was charged only with money laundering, meaning that monies from the Gambino criminal RICO enterprise were funneled to him. Nevertheless, the government also charged him with racketeering and racketeering conspiracy under RICO because it believed that the monies were given to him because he was either the acting or actual boss of the Gambino crime family. As such—under RICO—Peter was criminally accountable for all the crimes committed by all the other members of that enterprise, even though he did not commit any of them.

After Peter was convicted, I sentenced him to nine years. He was thereafter also indicted and convicted in the Southern District of New York for planning to kill Sammy the Bull—the notorious turncoat mafioso who testified against Peter's brother and put the proverbial nail in John Gotti's coffin. Peter was sentenced to twenty-five more years in jail, where he died at the age of eighty-two in 2021.

My Gotti trial was full of all sorts of *Godfather*-like moments and was a huge media frenzy. A few stand out to this day.

One day, after the three-month trial was well under way, I walked into the public elevator, going back to court after lunch. At that time there was no private judges' elevator because the courthouse was under renovation. I had no choice. It was either take the elevator or walk up ten flights of stairs to the courtroom. However, as the elevator door was closing, in walked "the Lump." He was the least culpable defendant, and I had let him stay at liberty on bail. His only alleged crime was that he helped one of the other defendants, who didn't weigh more than 150 pounds, collect an extortionate debt that was owed to the Gambino family. His role was simply to stand in the doorway of the victim's house— all 400 pounds of him—while his codefendant told the poor guy who opened the door that he "better pay up or else." Obviously, the Lump was the "else." The debt was paid on the spot.

Because he was out on bail, the Lump was free to come and go as he pleased. It was easier for him to take the elevator than to risk a heart attack by walking up the stairs. No one else came into the elevator. In one sense it was a good thing. The Lump took up so much space, anyone else would have had to squeeze in. I also thought of that guy who paid up as soon as he saw him. Sensing my discomfort, the Lump tried to put me at ease by telling me, "You'se a good judge. We all like you and have a lot of fuckin' respect for you. Otherwise, I would squash you like an ant."

Then there was the day when my wife-to-be, Betsy, came to court. There was not a day during the trial when the defendants' wives did not come. The lawyers had pointed them out to the jurors during the trial. It was the lawyers' way of showing that the wives supported their husbands. The wives sat together in the second row on the right side of the aisle. By contrast, the lawyers never mentioned the women sitting in the third row on the *left* side. They also came to court each day. They were considerably younger than the wives and generally more attractive: long blond hair, tight skirts, high heels. Many wore sunglasses. I remember from *The Godfather* movies how family oriented the mafiosi were. They would never divorce their wives and were admirably protective of their families. However, this did not prevent them from having women on the side. I was told by the court's marshals that they believed the gals in the third row were some of the defendants' girlfriends.

Betsy did not know this when she came into the courtroom during the first week of the trial to see what was happening. She unwittingly sat in the third row on the left side. In my biased opinion she was better looking than the women who surrounded her, but with her Cartier aviator sunglasses, long blond hair, high heels, and miniskirt she fit right in.

Months after the trial, I ran into Peter Gotti's lawyer Gerald Shargel at a bar association function. He told me that Betsy had created quite a stir. Peter's codefendants did not know who she belonged to. They thought that they knew all the girlfriends and were annoyed that someone was holding out. The ones who had girlfriends each swore that Betsy was not their other woman. No one believed anyone. One of them thought she must have been Peter's and accused him of cheating on his regular girlfriend.

Shargel finally made peace by telling the gang that the mystery woman was the judge's girlfriend. They were astonished—but they told Shargel that their respect for the judge just went right through the "fuckin' roof."

Peter did indeed have a girlfriend. I knew who she was because she introduced herself to me one day while I was having lunch at the local Greek diner. She told me her name was Marjorie Alexander and that she was the woman sitting every day on the far end of the third row. I told her that I could not talk to her, but she insisted on telling me that she and Peter had been together for many years and were madly in love with each other. Although I cut the conversation short, it did not end there. It seemed like every day I would get a letter from Marjorie telling me everything about her life with Peter and how much she was in love with him.

I was stunned when I learned that a few days after I had sentenced Peter, Marjorie committed suicide. She had checked into a Red Roof Inn in Nassau County earlier that day, taken a fistful of antidepressants, and tied a bag around her head. She left a note in the room apologizing to the hotel maid for any trouble she had caused. She had last been seen two days before speaking to a reporter about her public declarations of love for Peter. She told him, "I took a chance. Life is all about taking chances. Now, I am destroyed."

Even though the press was out in force during the trial, the media event that topped all else took place the day the famed kung fu movie star Steven Seagal took the stand. It was at the beginning of the fourth week of the trial. There were reporters all over the place—many in from Los Angeles—who were champing at the bit to write about Seagal's involvement with the Gambino family. The fifty-eighth and fifty-ninth counts of the indictment charged two of Peter Gotti's codefendants, Sonny Ciccone and Primo Cassarino, of conspiring to and attempting to extort money from the movie star. These were not the most important charges in the case—and had nothing to do with Peter or the Gambino family's control of the waterfront—but they certainly brought out the crowd.

Conscious of his public persona, Seagal—with his painted hairline and red necklaces—was clad in a chocolate-brown silk kimono, jeans, and construction boots. He testified that he was licensed to carry a gun and always carried one when he was in New York. I made sure that he did not have one with him in court.

Seagal had flown back for his court appearance from Thailand, where he was making his latest movie, *Belly of the Beast*. He described himself as an "actor, producer, director, musician, songwriter." At first, he was very combative, befitting a self-proclaimed martial arts expert. However, under aggressive cross-examination his testimony started to get shaky and evasive. "Listen to me," I firmly stated, "I don't have any experience in martial arts, but I have other powers here. Just listen to the question and answer it." I then took an early lunch break "so people [could] cool off a little bit."

When he came back to the courtroom for continued cross-examination, his tough-guy image was totally shattered. He brought two red shawls with him and asked me if he could place them over his lap to warm his chilly knees. The audience howled.

In his testimony, Seagal told the jury that he'd had a sit-down with Ciccone and Cassarino in a private room at Gage & Tollner, a popular restaurant in downtown Brooklyn. His onetime best friend and former producer Jules Nasso was with him. Nasso had ties to the Mafia and had enlisted Ciccone to resolve an ongoing dispute that Nasso had with Seagal over money that Nasso claimed the movie star owed him.

Seagal told the jurors that Ciccone began talking to him about "monies that [Seagal] owed Jules," and "went into the fact that he wanted [Seagal] to work with Jules." Seagal told Ciccone, "I'm trying," at which point Ciccone ordered, "Look at me when you are talking." Ciccone then said, "Look, we're proud people and work with Jules. . . . Jules is going to get a little and the pot will be split up. . . . We'll take a little."

The meeting ended with Seagal stating that he "would try to work with Jules." Seagal then testified that as he walked out of the restaurant, Nasso started walking with him and said, "You know, it's a good thing you said this and didn't say that because if you would have said the wrong thing, they were going to kill you."

Seagal also told the jurors that he had broken up his relationship with Nasso because Nasso was using mood-elevating drugs and "going into psychotic rages." Nonetheless, he testified that he paid Nasso between $500,000 and $700,000—he was not too good with numbers—after he had escaped with his life.

As Seagal recounted his real-life adventure, he seemed to regain his composure and warm to the audience. He began making dramatic faces—complete with his famous furrowed brow—in response to questions. He grinned at a juror. When he finished his testimony and I told him he could step down, he bowed twice to the crowd and said, "Thank you, all." The media event was over. It was time to get back to the rest of the trial.

I thought about the Peter Gotti trial as I read what the Probation Department had written in its presentence report to Judge Sifton about Anthony Russo's Mafia life and the crimes he and his codefendants had committed. Much of the information that judges gather before they impose a sentence is from the presentence report, together with written submissions from counsel. The presentence report is an indispensable sentencing tool. The Probation Department has the responsibility to gather as much relevant information as it can from a variety of sources about the defendant's criminal misdeeds and his past life. The defendant's counsel has the right to challenge what is contained in the presentence report and, if necessary, insist on a hearing to allow the court to assess its reliability. When I resentenced Russo, thirty years later, his attorney was satisfied that the information contained in the presentence report was largely accurate.

The presentence report before Judge Sifton gave me a ton of information about Russo, his Mafia connections, the nature of the crimes he had committed, and his personal life. It first told me that Russo was one of eleven codefendants. One, Alphonse Persico, was awaiting trial, one was a fugitive, and the other eight had entered into plea agreements and were awaiting sentence.

The presentence report told me that Russo was a captain of the Colombo crime family and gave me a riveting account of the murderous war that broke out between rival factions of the family back in the early 1990s. Much of what I recount here has been glorified in lots of Mafia movies, most notably the three *Godfather* movies. But it's necessary to understand Russo's role and life as a Colombo family mafioso.

The Colombo family is still part of a nationwide criminal organization. The ruling body of the organization is known as the Commission, whose members include the bosses of the five New York City–based families. In addition to the Colombo Family, the Commission includes representatives of the Genovese, Lucchese, Gambino, and Bonanno families, collectively known as La Cosa Nostra.

Each family has a similar internal organization, consisting of a head, also known as the boss, an underboss, and a counselor, also known as the consigliere. Beneath these three highest positions are the captains, or capos, who are also known as *caporegimes*, or "skippers." The capos are responsible for crews, which consist of "made" members. They are individuals who acquired their made-member status by committing serious crimes for their family—often murder—and have taken an oath of omertà, vowing never to reveal any information about the family.

The crew members are associates of the family and are known as soldiers and "good fellows." They produce funds from illegal activities, which are distributed throughout the family's hierarchy. In return for a percentage of the illegally derived funds, the highest-ranking members in the family provide services for the crew members, such as protection, and they settle disputes between organized crime members.

Carmine "Junior" Persico, also known as the Snake, had been the boss of the Colombo family for more than ten years when, in November 1986, he was sentenced to thirty-nine years in prison. In January 1987, he was sentenced to an additional one hundred years. Because of his imprisonment, in early 1987, Persico delegated the daily administration of Colombo family affairs to a handpicked committee of three of the family's high-ranking members. But in May 1988, Persico abandoned the committee system and selected Victor Orena as acting boss. Orena had been a member of the family for over twelve years and had been a captain for approximately one year before he became the acting boss.

But things did not go well between Persico and Orena, and by June 1991 a violent internal Colombo family war broke out. In the previous months, various members and associates of the Colombo family became increasingly disenchanted with Orena. They claimed that he demanded and retained too great a share of the money generated from the family's illegal activities. In addition, Orena announced his intention to become the official boss and to topple Persico as boss before Persico's son, Alphonse, was released from prison and could become the head of the family.

Thus, two Colombo family factions emerged, one aligned with Persico and the other with Orena. Each faction formed armed assassination teams to monitor the movements of the other faction and to assassinate its members and associates, as opportunities allowed. Blood flowed all over the streets of New York City.

Enter Anthony Russo. He was Persico's nephew and was related to other Persicos. In 1988, he had been appointed to the position of capo of the Colombo family by Orena and had his own crew. When the war broke out, Russo aligned himself with his Persico relatives and aided and abetted the activities of the Persico faction. On March 25, 1992, at his direction, his crew murdered John Minerva and Michael Imbergamo, who had become members of the rival Orena faction. Russo, with his crew, had been stalking them at a café owned by Minerva in Long Island. At approximately 10 p.m., Minerva and Imbergamo left the café after closing to go to their car. Before they got there, two members of Russo's assassination team fired several deadly shots at them. They both died sprawled on the street in pools of blood.

Under RICO, Russo was also held accountable for many other murders and attempted murders of members of the Orena faction by Russo's crew, which took place at his behest even though he didn't pull the triggers.

As for Russo's personal history, the presentence report revealed that he was a lifelong resident of Brooklyn, residing in the Park Slope section of the borough. His father, Sebastian Russo, had owned and operated a carting business in Brooklyn and died in 1977 from leukemia. His mother—a homemaker—was alive. Russo had three brothers, only one of whom was still living: Andrew was employed by the New York Sanitation Department. Joseph was shot in 1975, at the age of nineteen, and Robert died of a drug overdose in 1995, at the age of thirty-six.

Russo was married and had three sons. Sebastian, age twenty-one, was a stagehand for the Metropolitan Opera; Alfonse, age eighteen, was serving a sentence of three and a half to seven years in a Washington State correctional facility for assault; Joseph, age sixteen, was a student at Bishop Ford Central Catholic High School in Brooklyn. Russo's wife did not work. Russo lived with his family, including Alfonse when he was not in jail, in a two-family house on Third Street in Brooklyn. Russo left school after completing the ninth grade at John Jay High School in Brooklyn. He didn't take drugs and was in good physical health.

Because of his supervisory role in the murders of Minerva and Imbergamo by his assassination team and the many murders by his crew for which he was held accountable under RICO, Russo's total offense level was fifty points, far exceeding the forty-three-point base level for one murder. Judge Sifton had no discretion at that time but to impose a life sentence, even though Russo had never been incarcerated.

In 2023, Russo brought a motion before me for sentencing relief under the First Step Act. He was then seventy years old and had been in prison for his heinous crimes for thirty years. I studied the papers his lawyer had submitted in support of his application and brought Russo and his lawyer into my courtroom to listen to their arguments. When I returned to my chambers, I wasn't sure what I would do. He was responsible for many brutal murders, but was he entitled to a second chance?

5

THE MAFIA CASES: VITTORIO "LITTLE VIC" AMUSO

Vittorio Amuso was not a mere capo. He was the boss of the Lucchese crime family, one of La Cosa Nostra's Five Families. In 1992, he was sentenced to life by Judge Nickerson after a jury found Amuso guilty on each count of a fifty-four-count indictment. He was then fifty-seven years old. Assistant U.S. Attorney Charles Rose nicknamed Amuso "the Deadly Don."

The first count charged that between January 1978 and February 1992, as a leader of a racketeering enterprise, namely the Lucchese crime family ("LCF"), Amuso was accountable for the commission of forty-five racketeering acts. They ran the gamut from income tax evasion and extortions to drug trafficking and multiple murders.

While most of the murders were of mafiosi, not all were. One victim, Everett Hatcher, was a special agent of the Drug Enforcement Administration. Another, John Morrissey, was a union shop steward. Some of the murders were particularly gruesome. Michael Salerno, a prominent member of the Lucchese crime family's Bronx faction, who had visions of becoming the boss, was shot through the heart and stabbed in the throat. The one that became *Godfather* lore was the slaying of Bruno Facciolo, a suspected cooperator. After he was shot and stabbed to death, a dead canary was placed in his mouth as a warning from Amuso to potential informants. Al Visconti was then killed for planning to avenge Facciolo's death; in addition to being shot in the head, he was also shot in the groin because there were rumors that he was bisexual.

Amuso succeeded Anthony "Tony Ducks" Corallo as the Lucchese family boss in 1986 after Corallo was imprisoned. In 1988, Amuso promoted Anthony Casso from captain to consigliere, and two years later made him the underboss. Casso was named as a codefendant but was then a fugitive.

Amuso rarely dealt directly with his subordinates. As the boss, he had the sole authority to initiate new members into the family or to approve the murders of other La Cosa Nostra members. As underboss, Casso assisted Amuso in determining family policy, settling disputes, and governing all significant family actions. As his second-in-command, Casso delivered Amuso's directives to the various captains, who supervised the criminal activities of their crews.

Amuso stressed that the goal of the family was to generate income, which each member shared with the boss and his consigliere. Naturally, that income was never reported to the IRS. Amuso conducted all financial transactions in cash, maintained no bank accounts, and made numerous investments under others' names.

The income that the family members generated came from narcotics distribution, loan-sharking, and gambling, and through the family's widespread influence over unions in the trucking, garment, and construction industries. They exercised control over the New York City Housing Authority window replacement industry. Amuso was able to extort payoffs from many window manufacturers, such as American Aluminum and Visor Builders. Between 1987 and 1989, the family received $1 million as kickbacks for installed windows, of which 75% was retained by Amuso and Casso.

Amuso resorted to multiple murders to protect his position as boss. He would direct Casso to orchestrate them, but he never knew who carried out the assignments.

The Probation Department's presentence report gave very little information about Amuso's personal life. Although he met with the probation officer who prepared the report, Amuso shared very little with him. He acknowledged that he was married and had two children and that at the time of his arrest he was living in a house in Jamaica, Queens, with his spouse, children, and two stepdaughters.

Amuso's father was a tailor, and his mother was a homemaker. He said he had a good relationship with his family, although under marginal economic conditions. He had graduated from Brooklyn Automotive High School in 1951 and was in good health. On the advice of counsel, he declined to discuss his financial condition.

Amuso's lawyer was Gerald Shargel. For years Shargel was the Mafia's "go-to guy," and he would later brilliantly handle the Peter Gotti trial before me. Although his clientele left something to be desired, Shargel was well respected by the bench and bar. He eventually tired of representing "the boys" and navigating the pressure of resisting their unethical demands. His future clientele would be white-collar criminals.

Amuso had escaped long periods of incarceration before. When he was twenty, he spent two years in jail for burglary, and he spent several additional years behind bars when at twenty-six he was convicted for shooting a person—not fatally—while attempting to rob him. But Amuso's guidelines calculation in the RICO case came to a staggering total offense level of fifty-six, and Judge Nickerson had no choice but to sentence him to life.

* * *

Like Russo and all the other Mafia killers, Amuso was no stranger to guns, and he had also been charged and found guilty, in count twelve, of "Use of a Firearm During a Crime of Violence." The charge would not realistically have affected his life sentence, and I wondered, therefore, why the government even tacked it on, especially given the bizarre nature of our country's gun laws, where each state has its own gun laws and guns are a dime a dozen.

Much of the public's confusion about our gun laws is the byproduct of the compromise by the Founding Fathers—reflected in the Tenth Amendment—that permits each state to determine the nature and scope of criminal conduct within its borders, subject to overarching proscriptions by the federal government if interstate commerce is affected. Thus, in the absence of permissible federal interdiction, each state may decide for itself how, if at all, it will regulate the sale and possession of firearms.

Because Congress has declared that "the gun, its component parts, ammunition, and the raw materials from which they are made have considerably moved in interstate commerce," its power to regulate the sale and possession of guns could conceptually empower it to cover the entire field.[1] It has not, however, acted in this preemptive fashion, allowing state laws to govern in those areas not specifically proscribed by federal law. The federally proscribed guns are stolen firearms, firearms with obliterated serial numbers, machine guns, and firearms undetectable by metal detectors or X-ray machines.

In addition, some categories of people are federally prohibited from possessing any type of firearm: convicted felons, fugitives, unlawful users of controlled substances, "mental defectives," illegal aliens, those dishonorably discharged from the armed forces, anyone who has renounced his or her citizenship, those subject to restraining orders, anyone previously convicted of a misdemeanor domestic violence offense, and anyone who—like Amuso—possesses a firearm in furtherance of a crime of violence or drug trafficking. In addition, juveniles (i.e., those under the age of eighteen) are federally prohibited from possessing handguns but ironically may possess other guns that are not on the list of universally banned firearms—even military-style assault weapons.

What has Congress done to control criminals like Amuso, and what has it left to the states to do? Congress has passed a few significant statutes, and Amuso was indicted under the one proscribing the use or possession of a firearm during drug trafficking or some other violent crime. The statute provides for significant jail time, to run consecutive to other related sentences.

The statute also made it a crime for any convicted felon to possess a gun. Thus, regardless of where that person was found and the nature of the previous felony, the defendant would be guilty of a federal gun crime. These prosecutions are commonplace in the federal courts. I have had my fair share, and they invariably result in putting the defendant behind bars for a couple of years. I'm sympathetic, however, to many of these former convicts. They live in dangerous neighborhoods where everyone carries a gun for their own protection. If I lived there, I probably would also carry one. Nonetheless, it is a punishable federal crime.

To be sure, Congress has made some efforts to control the sale of guns lest they wind up in the hands of the likes of Amuso, but these efforts have not been terribly effective. The 1968 Gun Control Act required gun dealers to be licensed; however, those "not engaged in the business" of selling firearms, or who make only "occasional" sales, were exempt. Thus, as a practical matter, under what has commonly become known as the "gun show loophole," federal law does not preclude unlicensed sellers from selling privately owned firearms at gun shows or other temporary locations.

In 1983, Congress passed the Brady Act, requiring those covered by the Gun Control Act to secure a background check on the putative purchaser to ensure that he or she was not a prohibited person under one of the proscribed categories; however, those within the so-called gun show loophole, who were not covered by the Gun Control Act, could still sell firearms without a background check. Notably, although the states were free to plug the loophole, thirty-two states have not done so. Thus, in those states, no licensing or background checks are required of the private or occasional seller of firearms.

Other than these minimal federal restrictions, the states are free to do as they please—so long as they do not violate the Second Amendment. Notably, in the landmark *Heller* case, the Supreme Court held that the Second Amendment was not limited to the militia; rather, it included the right of individuals to bear arms in their homes for self-defense.

With fifty states each weighing in on what is otherwise legal or illegal, it is no wonder the public may be confused. For example, in forty states assault weapons can legally be bought.[2] Forty-five states have no limit on the number of guns that can be purchased in one month, while four states impose a limit of one handgun per month.[3] In addition, because federal law bars juveniles from possessing handguns only, rather than all firearms, juvenile possession of long guns is legal in many states.[4] It puzzles me, for example, that a twelve-year-old in North Carolina, although needing parental permission to play Little League Baseball, does not need permission to possess any type of shotgun or rifle, which would include semiautomatic assault rifles.[5]

Many states, however, do require licenses for the possession of firearms that are not illegal under federal law. For example, since I am not a prohibited person under federal law, and the possession of handguns is not *federally* proscribed, I can legally buy a handgun without a license in many states, but I cannot possess one in New York without a New York license.

The maze of state gun laws, ranging from states such as Maine, which has virtually no gun control laws, to Massachusetts and Hawaii, which have highly restrictive laws, and the many variations in between from state to state, makes it impossible for the average person to know when or where in the United States the possession of a firearm is legal—let alone which type of firearm—without consulting a lawyer or the NRA. Thus, the gun-carrying citizen traveling across state lines may be lawfully in possession of the firearm in one state but not in the other, unwittingly being exposed to criminal prosecution. Therefore, even if New York Giant's football star Plaxico Burress was lawfully licensed to possess a handgun in his home in New Jersey, this was no defense to the gun possession charges he faced under New York law—which landed him in prison for two years.

To guard against this, the NRA has published a *Guide to the Interstate Transportation of Firearms* explaining the caveats gun carriers face in their interstate travels.[6] Congress has also addressed the problem by providing that a firearm may be transported from one state, in which the firearm may be lawfully possessed, to a non-contiguous state, thereby insulating the transporter from the laws of the states in between where the possession of the firearm may be illegal. Nonetheless, the interstate traveler may not be aware that the statute contains a number of qualifications: the firearm must be unloaded; neither the firearm nor any ammunition can be "readily accessible or . . . directly accessible from the passenger compartment of [the] transporting vehicle"; and if the vehicle does not have a compartment separate from the driver's compartment, the firearm or ammunition "shall be contained in a locked container other than the glove compartment or console."

Despite (or because of) this panoply of regulations, it has been estimated that 44% of U.S. households contain guns.[7] Moreover, our appetite for guns has been on the rise.[8] FBI statistics show that there were 31 million requests for background checks of potential gun buyers throughout the nation in 2022—more than double the number of requests in 2010.[9]

And our country's gun culture has been bolstered by the effective lobbying efforts of the NRA to keep Congress at bay. The result is the highest rate of gun deaths in the developed world. And the relative numbers are startling. For example, while 2019 numbers for all firearm-related deaths show New Zealand having had 48; Sweden, 152; Australia, 241; the United Kingdom, 162; and Canada, 875; the United States had 37,040.[10] Even adjusted for population disparities, the differentials are palpable: U.S. gun homicides per 100,000 residents was "26 times that of other high-income countries."[11]

New York Times columnist Bob Herbert reported that in 2009 there were 283 million privately owned firearms in America; someone was killed by a gun in our country every 17 minutes; 8 American children were shot to death every day; and since the fateful September 11 attacks against the United States, "nearly 120,000 Americans had been killed in non-terror homicides, most of them committed with guns." This was "nearly 25 times the Americans killed in Iraq and Afghanistan." Herbert further noted that nearly 70,000 Americans were shot nonfatally each year, leading to "well more than $2 billion annually" in medical costs.[12] Currently, according to Small Arms Survey, an independent research project in Switzerland, the United States, with 4% of the world's population, possesses about 40% of the world's firearms, and there are an estimated 393 million privately held firearms in our country—more than one per person and more than the top twenty-five countries in the world combined.[13]

Gun sales and gun-related deaths have only escalated since Herbert's article, capped today by the proliferation of mass murders. As reported by Kiara Alfonseca for *ABC News* on September 5, 2023, there had been five mass shootings in the United States in just the first four days of that month. She also reported that, according to the Gun Violence Archive, there were at least 484 shootings in the United States in the first eight months of 2023, averaging almost two a day.[13]

The impact of mass shootings on our country's communities has been profound. The Gun Violence Archive, a nonprofit that catalogs every incidence of gun violence in the United States, has defined a mass shooting as an incident in which four or more victims are shot or killed.

The list since the beginning of 2023 is staggering. In addition to Maine, Dallas, Nashville, Buffalo, and Uvalde, there were mass murders in such places as Birmingham, Alabama; Washington, DC; Philadelphia, Pennsylvania; Fort Worth, Texas; Baltimore, Maryland; Atlanta, Georgia; Cleveland, Texas; Dadeville, Alabama; Louisville, Kentucky; Michigan State University; Oakland, California; Half Moon Bay, California; Monterey Park, California; Enoch City, Utah; and Huntsville, Alabama.[14]

Undoubtedly, by the time this book is published, there will be many more. Tragically, we are becoming inured to the weekly drumbeat of the uniquely American phrase "mass murder," which is sadly contributing to a growing international reputation that the United States may be the most violent country in the world. Indeed. Canada, the UK, France, New Zealand, Australia, Venezuela, and Uruguay have issued travel advisories about visiting the United States because of our gun violence.[15]

Surely, Amuso and the Mafia had no trouble getting whatever guns they needed for their murderous deeds.

6

THE MAFIA CASES:
ANTHONY "GASPIPE" CASSO

It was no accident that Casso's nickname was "Gaspipe"; as the *New York Post* reported, "An investigator who covered Casso's cases described him as 'a ruthless homicidal maniac who enjoyed killing.'"[1]

In 1991, Sammy "the Bull" Gravano agreed to testify against John Gotti after hearing the Gambino boss make several disparaging remarks about Gravano on a wiretap that implicated both the men in several murders. The most notorious was the slaying of former Gambino boss Paul Castellano outside Sparks Steak House. It paved the way for Gotti to succeed Castellano and for the Bull to become the underboss of the Gambino crime family.

At that time, Gravano was the highest-ranking member of the Five Families to break his blood oath of omertà and cooperate with the government. As a result, in 1992 the Teflon Don was finally convicted of murder and sentenced by Judge I. Leo Glasser to life without parole.

Gravano and Casso had been indicted for an assortment of

violent crimes, including numerous murders, and were also destined to spend the rest of their lives behind bars. However, because of Gravano's profound cooperation, which dealt a devastating blow to the Mafia, Judge Glasser rewarded him with a five-year sentence. At that time, Gravano had been in jail for four years, and with credit for time served he would soon be a free man.

Seeing the handwriting on the wall, Casso became the second mafioso to break the oath of silence. Under his cooperation agreement he had to tell everything he knew at proffer sessions with the prosecutors about the criminal misdeeds of his fellow mafiosi and to testify against them at any trials. But he also had to plead guilty to all the many charges against him, including multiple murders. In exchange, the government would file with the judge what is known in the trade as a §5K1 letter, apprising the judge of Casso's cooperation. The judge would then have the power to reward Casso for his cooperation by imposing a lenient sentence, as Judge Glasser did for Sammy the Bull.

But the cooperation agreement—like all cooperation agreements—contained one huge caveat: Casso had to be truthful with the government. If he lied or if the government in good faith was not satisfied with his behavior, the government had the right to tear up the agreement. Casso would then be sentenced for all the crimes to which he pled. Because of all the murders, it would be life.

Cooperation agreements are the number one tool the government has in its prosecutorial arsenal. About 10% of all federal defendants have cooperation deals.[2] Without them, many convictions for serious crimes would never happen. The theory is simple: the government uses a "little fish" to catch a bigger one. Sometimes the little fish is not so little, like Gravano and Casso, but their cooperation is key to accomplishing a major government objective—like taking down the Mafia.

On March 1, 1994, Gaspipe Casso appeared before Judge Nickerson to enter his guilty pleas. The judge carefully reviewed the cooperation agreement with him to make sure he knew what was at stake. Casso then pled guilty to seventy counts of the indictment. But before Judge Nickerson could accept his pleas, Casso was required under the law to explain what he did.

Casso had been briefed by his lawyer that he would have to fully fess up. He read from prepared notes. First, he admitted that he "held various positions in the Lucchese Crime Family, including associate member, consigliere and underboss." He then explained why he was guilty of every count, including fifteen murder counts. In that respect, he confessed to "ordering subordinate members and associates of the Lucchese Crime Family to carry out these murders, and which, in fact, were attempted or carried out."

He then named the victims: Angelo Sigona, Michael Pappadio, Julius Calder, John Petrucelli, John "Sonny" Morrissey, Joe LaMorte, Joseph Martinelli, Michael Salerno, Bruno Facciolo, Larry Taylor, Al Visconti, Peter Chiodo, Anthony Fava, Robert Kubecka, and Donald Barstow.

Judge Nickerson must have sat in disbelief as Gaspipe rattled off this laundry list.

During debriefings before two of the government's lead prosecutors, Charles Rose and Valerie Caproni, Casso named scores of other mobsters he had conspired with, including Genovese boss Vincent Gigante. Casso also confessed to having sent hit men to Assistant U.S. Attorney Rose's home to murder *him*. While Rose was prosecuting Casso, a story regarding Casso's wife was printed by the press, and Casso believed that Rose had leaked the story. Consequently, Casso ordered two corrupt New York City police officers and a fellow mafioso to find Rose's residence and murder him. Several efforts were made to locate Rose; however, the would-be murderers never found him, and Rose escaped with his life.

Casso also admitted to plotting to assassinate Judge Nickerson to force a mistrial. According to Casso, he discussed the judge's murder with members of the Lucchese and Colombo families. Casso learned which commuter train was used by Judge Nickerson and told the would-be assassins. The plan involved murdering Judge Nickerson in the vicinity of the train station. Fortunately, it never happened.

Because Judge Nickerson believed he could no longer be impartial, he recused himself.

I drew the black bead.

The government then decided to pull the plug on Casso's cooperation agreement. The prosecutors put forth reasons why he had breached it, but one of the government's lawyers had told a reporter, "It gets to a point where somebody is just too evil to put on the stand."[3] Casso then made a motion before me for "specific performance" to require the government to adhere to its agreement.

The government contended that it was not obligated to adhere to its bargain because "Casso committed crimes during the term of his cooperation agreement." For his part, Casso argued that the government was acting in bad faith because his "conduct did not constitute a material breach of the cooperation agreement, that the government's stated reasons for abrogating the cooperation agreement [were] a pretext, and that the government entered into the agreement with the intent to breach it at a later time."

Casso further supported his contention that the government had acted in "bad faith" by claiming:

> (1) his proffer session was unusually brief; (2) the government never allowed him to prove himself as a prosecution witness and would not permit him to testify at a State criminal trial in Kings County; (3) the

government has not followed up on leads he provided; (4) agents from the Drug Enforcement Administration have never interviewed him; (5) the Office has repeatedly leaked information from Casso to the press; (6) the Office has warned other cooperating witnesses to stay away from him; (7) a prosecutor stated in 1995 that he believed that Casso could not be used as a witness; and (8) a former prosecutor, discussing the trial of Vincent Gigante with the *New York Times* several months before Gigante's trial took place, did not mention Casso as a potential witness.

The government gave three reasons for its decision to withdraw the deal: "(1) while imprisoned, Casso had assaulted another inmate; (2) Casso had participated in the smuggling of contraband into prison, and had bribed prison officials as part of this scheme; and (3) Casso had fabricated false information regarding the testimony of two other cooperating witnesses, Alphonse D'Arco ('D'Arco') and Salvatore Gravano ('Gravano')."

The government conceded that Casso had given substantial assistance to law enforcement authorities but argued that "Casso's undisputed commission of crimes while in prison and his alleged fabrication of information regarding D'Arco and Gravano constitute breaches of the cooperation agreement that relieve the government from its contractual duty to file a §5K1 motion."

Casso admitted that he assaulted another inmate and that he bribed prison guards to smuggle contraband into the jail, but he claimed that the government had singled him out for punishment "and that other inmates have engaged in similar conduct without having their cooperation agreements terminated." He also claimed that he was being punished "for providing information that calls into question the credibility of Gravano and D'Arco."

* * *

I read both sides' briefs carefully and wrote an extensive written opinion. I concluded that Casso had not effectively shown that the government did not intend to honor the agreement at its inception.[4] And I pointed out the irrationality of Casso's argument that others who have committed comparable or even more serious crimes "have not been treated as harshly as he." I agreed that "the new crimes, when considered together with the 15 murders to which Casso confessed, are not realistically likely to have an impact upon his credibility" but concluded that ignoring them would lead to perverse and counterintuitive results, "since the more egregious a defendant's criminal history, the less likely it is that the commission of crimes during the term of a cooperation agreement will have an ascertainable impact upon the defendant's credibility." In sum, I concluded that Casso's commission of other crimes during his incarceration gave the government a good-faith basis for its honest dissatisfaction with his performance.

Thus, on June 29, 1998, I denied Casso's motion, which meant I would have to sentence Anthony "Gaspipe" Casso to life imprisonment.

As I expected, Casso appealed, and in April of the following year, the circuit court affirmed my decision. I was happy to put Casso behind me and return to my other judicial work. I hoped that I never would have to hear about him again.

But was I wrong!

He was ushered into my chambers a few weeks later by my courtroom deputy, Mike Innelli. The FBI special agent looked right out of central casting—tall and handsome, with short-cropped hair. The American flag pin in the left lapel of his dark blue suit sparkled.

He went right to the point and told me that the FBI and the Marshals Service investigated over three hundred threats against federal judges annually. This meant that about one-third of the circuit and district judges were yearly at risk of bodily harm and death. I told him that when I took the job, I had no idea the risk level would be so high.

The agent explained that it was the policy and practice of the FBI and the Marshals Service to tell the judges at once about any threats and to ensure that the threats would be seriously and promptly investigated. After the investigation was completed, a threat-level assessment would be made. It would be either a low threat level, a potential danger level, or a serious threat level. The judge would, of course, be kept abreast of everything that was happening.

I thanked the agent for giving me the good news that Casso wanted to kill me. He tried to calm me by telling me that the threat was picked up through the jailhouse rumor mill and probably would not amount to much. Nonetheless, it would be seriously checked out. He would be in touch with me as the investigation unfolded.

I asked him if there was anything I should do in the meantime. He just told me to be careful. He also asked whether I would like to carry a gun. I told him that I had never shot one and would probably shoot myself by mistake.

A few months later, the FBI special agent returned and told me that Casso's death threat had been classified as low risk. There was no tangible evidence that any contract had been placed on my life, and since Casso was in a maximum security prison for the rest of his life, there was no risk that he could kill me—so long as he did not escape or I disregarded his lifetime sentence and set him free. I assured him that under the law—at that time—that could never happen.

Since then, I have had two other death threats by other less-than-model characters. They, too, were classified as low risk, but the message was clear—being a judge was no bed of roses. You were truly in the service of your country, and—just as in combat—you could lose your life.

After the agent left, I educated myself about the level of death threats against my fellow federal judges. As reported in an August 15, 2023, *Time* magazine article, "[t]hreats against federal judges [had] spiked 400% in the past six years, to more than 3,700 in 2022, according to the U.S. Marshals Service."[5]

I learned that if Casso had his way, I would be the fifth federal judge to be assassinated during the prior two decades.

John H. Wood Jr., a district judge for the Western District of Texas, was assassinated on May 29, 1979, by Charles Harrelson—the father of the actor Woody Harrelson. It was a contract killing orchestrated by the Texas drug lord Jamiel Chagra, who was waiting to be tried before Judge Wood. As a reminder of the dangers that judges face, the San Antonio federal courthouse now bears his name.

Richard J. Daronco was a district judge closer to home. He sat on the Southern District bench in Manhattan. Judge Daronco was assassinated on May 21, 1988, by the father of a civil plaintiff whose case was dismissed by the judge. He was shot while mowing his lawn in front of his home.

Robert Smith Vance, a judge for the Eleventh Circuit Court of Appeals, was assassinated on December 16, 1989, when he opened a package containing a bomb, which immediately exploded. The package was the handiwork of Walter Leroy Moody Jr., who had lost his appeals before that appellate court from his criminal conviction for possessing another bomb. Ironically, Judge Vance had nothing to do with the case; he was neither the trial judge nor on the appellate panel that affirmed Moody's conviction.

John Roll was a district judge in Arizona when he was a victim of a mass shooting that seriously wounded Arizona congresswoman Gabby Giffords. A dozen others were also wounded in the attack, which left six people dead, including Judge Roll. He had earlier attended mass and decided at the last minute to spend some time at the Giffords event.

Judges' families are also at risk. On February 29, 2005, Judge Joan Lefkow returned home late in the evening after a long day on the bench. Unbeknownst to her, Bart Ross, a disgruntled plaintiff in a medical malpractice case that the judge had tossed out of court, had learned where she lived and had gone there earlier in the night to kill her. When the judge arrived, Ross was nowhere in sight, but she found her mother and husband in the basement. They had been murdered.

Judge Lefkow had also been the target of threats five years earlier from Matthew Hale, a white supremacist. The judge had enjoined him from using the name he had chosen for his organization. Hale was subsequently sentenced to a forty-year prison term for soliciting an undercover informant to kill her.

A similar fate befell Judge Esther Salas's family. In July 2020, her husband and son were gunned down at the family's New Jersey home. Her husband survived, but her son did not. Nina Totenberg of NPR reported:

> [Judge] Salas remembers the night of the attack on her family with horrible clarity. . . . She and her son [Daniel] were in the basement cleaning up after his twentieth birthday party. And they were talking. "I remember him saying, 'Mom, let's keep talking. I love talking to you, Mom.' And at that exact moment, the doorbell rang . . . and before I could say anything, he just shot up the stairs," Salas recalls. The next thing she heard was her husband screaming, "No!" followed by loud bangs. So loud that, as she raced upstairs, she thought a bomb had gone off. What she found was "just as gruesome."

"There was my son . . . holding his chest, and my husband, who I didn't know was bleeding out, who had literally crawled to the front porch to see if he could see any identifying features of the car. And he's screaming, 'Call 911. Call 911.'"

Daniel was pronounced dead at the hospital. Her husband had been shot three times but miraculously survived after undergoing multiple surgeries. Daniel was Judge Salas's only child. Before he was born, she'd had three miscarriages. She referred to "Danny" as her "karma baby," and thanked God every day for that blessing. It was their religious faith that got her and her husband through that incomprehensible tragedy. And because of their faith, they eventually forgave that warped killer and felt "lighter" for doing that.[6]

As Totenberg further reported:

The shooter, later identified as seventy-two-year-old lawyer Roy Den Hollander, was found after he killed himself. He had appeared once before Judge Salas, months earlier, and she had postponed ruling on his case at the request of the government. "He was angry with me for being a woman," Salas says. "He was angry with me for being Latina."

Hollander, a self-proclaimed antifeminist, had been active in a men's rights group. The FBI later matched his gun to the murder of a rival in that group in California. Found in Hollander's rental car was a list of potential targets, including three other female judges. Also discovered was the latest online publication of his manifesto, in which Hollander railed about discrimination against men.[7]

Judge Salas turned her energies to lobbying for significant security reforms for federal judges and their families. Two years after the attacks, Congress passed a bill shielding identifiable information of federal judges and their immediate families.[8] The legislation barred "disclosure of their home addresses, Social Security numbers, contact information, photos of their homes and vehicles, and the names of schools and employers of immediate family members."[9]

Hollander was an active criminal defense lawyer practicing before the federal district courts in New York as well as in New Jersey. He had appeared before me several times without incident, even though I had never ruled in his favor.

But there was a frightening incident that did occur in my courtroom. On March 11, 2008, Victor Wright was brought to court to be sentenced by me to life after having been convicted of serious drug crimes. He seemed to accept his incipient fate because he had not shown any signs of hostility at any prior time he had been before me. But not on this occasion. As he walked into my courtroom—followed closely by two marshals—he bolted past his attorney, razor in hand, and lunged at the prosecutor Carolyn Pokorny, a thirty-eight-year-old assistant U.S. attorney. He started to choke her.

Mayhem broke loose. But within seconds, Ron Tolkin, the court reporter, who was nearby, and the marshals jumped on Wright. The razor fell to the ground, and the marshals were on the verge of inflicting a deadly choke hold on the defendant when Wright took his hands off Pokorny's throat.

I sat frozen and startled, but I did not leave the bench to try to help. All the judges had been instructed during periodic security briefings not to interfere with the trained marshals, which could make matters worse.

The incident was captured on tape by the monitors that are in every courtroom and was shown on national TV that night. The video has become a training tool for the Marshals Service. It also raised a debate as to how best to guard against future violent courtroom episodes. And all hell was raised as to how the defendant was able to bring a razor into the courtroom.

A 2009 *Washington Post* article by Jerry Markon reported that threats to federal judges and prosecutors were then on the rise. He attributed the trend to "disgruntled defendants whose anger is fueled by the Internet; terrorism and gang cases that bring more violent offenders into federal court; frustration at the economic crises; and the rise of the 'sovereign citizens' movement—a loose collection of tax protesters, white supremacists and others who don't respect federal authority."[10] His comments were prescient.

There are, in short, a lot of "loose screws" out there. Harold Turner was one of them. Since 2001, Turner had been broadcasting an incendiary internet radio show from his home studio in North Bergen, New Jersey, gaining notoriety for his anti-immigrant and anti-Semitic remarks. Turner was arrested in 2010 for making death threats against three circuit court judges from Chicago. He took exception to a decision that they had rendered upholding a handgun ban and posted a message on his website expressing his outrage. He called the judges "cunning, ruthless, untrustworthy, disloyal, unpatriotic, deceitful scum."

The free speech clause of the First Amendment of the Constitution gave him the right to make these obnoxious comments, but he did not stop there. He went on to write, "These judges deserve to be killed," and "If they are allowed to get away with this by surviving, other judges will act the same way." To make matters worse, he posted their home addresses and photos.

Turner was convicted for his frightening conduct. A jury in my courthouse—where the case was tried—determined that he had crossed the line that the First Amendment draws; you can't yell "fire" in a crowded theater. Turner was sentenced to three years in jail, but the three judges he wanted dead must wonder if some kook out there might be hiding in wait for them or their families, urged on by Turner's words.

In some courts throughout the country, every defendant brought into a courtroom who is in custody is cuffed; some are also shackled. I handled a few sentences several years ago as a visiting judge in the New Orleans federal courthouse. One of the defendants had been incarcerated for a few months. I sentenced him to time served for possessing a small quantity of drugs. His family was in the courtroom, including his uncle, who was a local sheriff. The defendant was hardly a threat, yet he stood before me in handcuffs. I was told that the judges had no say in the matter. It was simply the policy of the district's chief marshal.

We do not do this in my district. While security has been tightened because of the Victor Wright and Harold Turner incidents, there is no "one-cuff-fits-all" policy. With rare exceptions, I do not allow defendants to be handcuffed while I sentence them. Perhaps I should, but I think it is demeaning and dehumanizing. However, I am no hero. If the defendant is being sentenced for a violent crime, I make sure the marshal's office knows that, and I will require the defendant to sit at his counsel's table—with the marshals right behind him—so that he is not close to me and the prosecutors.

Security is also of concern in other respects. Everyone entering the two Eastern District of New York courthouses must be screened by a metal detector—even the lawyers and court personnel. In addition, the public is not allowed to bring cell phones into the buildings. They must be checked at the marshal's desk at the entrances. But there is no uniformity throughout the country. Each district adopts its own cell phone policy.

The no-cell-phone policy at my courthouse used to apply to the lawyers also, but it was changed several years ago at the insistence of the judges. We did not deem it to be a security risk. We thought that lawyers' cell phones were an essential tool of the lawyers' trade and that they should have ready access to them. One restriction was imposed, however: they had to be shut off while the lawyer was in the courtroom. Some of my colleagues were concerned that lawyers would forget to do that and ringing cell phones would become a distraction. Their fears turned out to be unfounded. On only one occasion has a cell phone gone off in my courtroom. It was mine.

The state judiciaries have hardly been immune from violent attacks from disgruntled litigants. In the same year that Judge Lefkow's mother and husband were killed, shootings outside the local courthouse in Tyler, Texas, left two people dead and four others wounded. A judge, courtroom reporter, and deputy sheriff were also murdered that year in the Fulton County courthouse in Atlanta, Georgia. And sadly, on October 21, 2023, fifty-two-year-old Maryland Circuit Court Judge Andrew Wilkinson was shot to death in his driveway after the judge had awarded custody of the killer's children to his ex-wife.

On January 3, 2024, Deobra Delone Redden jumped over the courtroom bench of Nevada Clark County District Court Judge Mary Kay Holthus as she was about to sentence him to jail to give him "a taste of something else" other than his freedom for an attempted battery. He landed on top of the judge and slammed her head against a wall before he was pulled away. Judge Holthus was taken to a hospital where she was treated for her injuries, which fortunately proved not to be serious, and was back in the courtroom the next day. The judge ultimately sentenced Redden to four years.

He had told officers searching him after the attack that he had intended to kill her.[11]

Recently, the four indictments against Donald Trump have put judges and law enforcement officers at more risk than at any time in the history of our nation. Rightly or wrongly, his "base" believes he is unjustly being persecuted for nefarious political reasons, and death threats are commonplace.

Soon after the former president's residence at Mar-a-Lago was searched by FBI agents in the summer of 2022, a man wearing body armor and carrying an AR-15 rifle tried to break into an FBI office in Cincinnati after posting online that he wanted to kill agents. He was killed in a standoff with the police.

A week later, a Utah man named Craig Deleeuw Robertson was fatally shot by FBI agents when they attempted to arrest him after he repeatedly threatened to kill New York district attorney Alvin Bragg and President Biden. At that time, Rachel Kleinfeld, who studies polarization and political violence at the Carnegie Endowment for International Peace, told *Time* magazine: "There's enough precedent now of having those threats become real that [federal agents] have to take them seriously, which takes a huge amount of federal resources." She added, "This is the tip of an iceberg. We're going to need as a democracy to spend more to protect the rest of our servants if we refuse to take down the temperature."[12]

Since then, things have only escalated. For example, in the summer of 2023, a Texas woman was arrested because she sent a threatening and racist voicemail to the federal judge in Washington, DC, who was randomly assigned to oversee the Justice Department's election interference case against Trump. Her voicemail said, "You are in our sights, we want to kill you." She added that if Trump were not elected president in 2024, "[W]e are coming to kill you," and "[Y]ou will be targeted personally, publicly, your family, all of it."[13]

Lay public citizens doing their civic duty have also been targeted. A fringe website known for extreme rhetoric posted online the addresses and phone numbers of grand jurors after they voted to indict Trump in Georgia for election interference.

Closer to home, District Judge James Robart, of the Western District of the state of Washington, "received more than one hundred death threats after ruling against the Trump administration's first travel ban in February 2017." As the American Bar Association reported, "Most threats came after the president called Robart 'a so-called judge' and tweeted: 'Just cannot believe a judge would put our country in such peril. If something happens, blame him and court system.'"[14]

There is not a judge who has been randomly charged with presiding over a Trump indictment or civil proceeding who has not been the subject of Trump's vitriol. His ubiquitous efforts to condemn the judges to animate his hostile base have a chilling effect on the country's dedicated judges trying to uphold their oath to apply the rule of law.

According to a February 2024 report from Reuters, the U.S. Marshals Service has become increasingly concerned about a "rising tide of threats" against federal judges and prosecutors "fueled by partisan divisions and vitriol on social media." U.S. Marshals director Ronald Davis cited a growing number of threats against judges deemed serious enough to trigger an investigation, with such threats more than doubling from fiscal year 2021 to fiscal year 2023: from 224 to 457 incidents. As Davis remarked, "The threat environment right now that is causing me concern is when people disagree with the judicial process or the government, and that turns into those verbal attacks. And that is the beginning of the process that threatens the judiciary and threatens our democracy."[15]

So far, I have been unscathed. But I did recently dodge one bullet. A police officer who had been fired by the NYPD for cavorting with Trump's convicted buddy Roger Stone during the January 6 U.S. Capitol attack sued the NYPD, claiming his First Amendment rights had been violated. I denied the police department's motion to dismiss his complaint, holding that he had alleged a viable constitutional claim.[16] I was amused that Fox News had favorable comments to make that night about my ruling.

While I had no idea what was in store for me when I took the oath of office three decades ago, I have somehow—without undue fear—taken it all with a fatalistic grain of salt. But twenty-two years after I sentenced him to life, should I have granted Casso's compassionate release motion—even though he apparently wanted to kill me—when he was now a feebleminded, terminally ill old man who just wanted to die at home?

PART II
THE LAW

7

THE FIRST STEP ACT

The First Step Act became the law of the land on December 21, 2018. How did this major sentencing-reform bill come to pass when the politically charged mantra of most members of Congress was, and remains, to be tough on crime? And why was the bill signed into law by President Trump, whose "base" has led the charge for putting more people behind bars?

As a *Vox* article from 2020 recounts, before he signed the bill, the president supported his base's call for stricter sentencing laws and "promoted 'tough on crime' policies not just since his run for president in 2016, but in the decades before. In 1989, Trump ran a local ad calling for the death penalty for the 'Central Park Five,' who were falsely accused of attacking and raping a jogger in New York City."[1] Fortunately, Trump did not prevail, since all five were exonerated after spending years in jail, and one of them, Yusef Salaam, has recently been elected to the New York City council. Trump wrote in his 2000 book *The America We Deserve* that "[t]ough on crime policies are the most important form of national defense" and "[c]learly we don't have too many people in prison. Quite the contrary."[2]

Nonetheless, in supporting the First Step Act he did a flip-flop and portrayed himself as a profound sentencing reformer. He commented that his "job is to fight for all citizens, even those who have made mistakes" and that the act "brings much-needed hope to many families during the holiday season."[3]

This reflected a major pivot by the GOP and Trump's prior punitive, law-and-order stance. One criminal justice expert, Rachel Barkow, a professor at New York University Law School, expressed the view of many who were surprised by Trump's embrace of the First Step Act and his support of sentencing reform as "just the outlier on what would otherwise be a truly abysmal record on criminal justice issues."[4]

Her thoughts rang true with journalist Maggie Haberman, a White House correspondent for the *New York Times*. Haberman recently wrote for the paper in a political memo that Trump was "flaunting" the First Step Act, his "signature criminal justice reform law," to "help increase support among Black voters and potentially swing the election."

In her article, Haberman explained that Trump had recently met with Michael Harris, a high-profile Black celebrity and the founder of Death Row Records, who had been pardoned by the president on his last full day in office after Harris had served decades in prison.

Although Harris would not discuss what transpired at their meeting, Haberman reported that "he expressed gratitude toward the Trump administration in a statement and praised the sentencing law."

But not everyone approved of Trump's support for the First Step Act. According to Haberman, he "soured" on it "soon after signing it" because of criticism he received from a number of hard-core Republicans and conservative associates.

In Haberman's words, although Trump had "grown increasingly violent in his rhetoric about crime in America, saying that he
admires the freedom that despots have to execute drug dealers and
that shoplifters should be shot on the spot," he viewed the law "as
something that should have won him support from Black voters."
He boasted that he "did it for African Americans," when asked
about his repeated expressions of regret about the act. "Nobody else
could have gotten it done. Got zero credit."

Thus, as Haberman writes, "one difficulty in holding Mr. Trump
to account is that he often has a contradictory set of words and
actions that different people can latch onto," which allows "different people to read what they want into his behavior and will happily
play to whatever audience he's in front of."

Haberman quotes Michael Waldman, the president and chief
executive of the Brennan Center for Justice during Clinton's presidency, that although Trump was "bloodthirsty in his rhetoric," he
nonetheless did sign the First Step Act: "Whether he truly believed
it or not, he did it."

In the same week that Harris met with Trump, the president
received a call from Alice Johnson. Her life sentence on charges
related to cocaine possession had been commuted by Trump after
a meeting between Trump and celebrities Kanye West and his
wife, Kim Kardashian, both outspoken sentence-reform advocates.
Recounting her conversation with the president, Johnson said, "My
whole conversation was just encouragement" about the criminal
justice reform bill. Johnson later spoke at the Republican National
Convention in 2020. She said that no one had asked her to call
Trump or engage in politics for him, but added, "[H]e actually is
proud of that piece of legislation."

Thus, there are inconsistent views of Trump's criminal justice
positions. As Haberman mused, "It remains to be seen how willing
Mr. Trump will be, if at all, to speak about the criminal justice law"

and "whether Mr. Harris might be asked to speak publicly." Trump will have those opportunities during the presidential campaign.[5]

But Donald Trump is not the only one in the political crosshairs. In a lengthy guest essay in the *New York Times* on December 29, 2023, entitled "How Biden Can Tackle Mass Incarceration," Michael Romano, who chairs California's Committee on Revision of the Penal Code, took the president to task: "Despite historical bipartisan support for sentencing reform, Mr. Biden has failed to fully embrace the momentum of his two immediate predecessors, who made substantial efforts to tackle mass incarceration." He added that "[s]ome have argued that his relative inaction on the issue may hurt him among key voting groups."

Romano, who is the founder and director of the Three Strikes Project at Stanford Law School, which represents people sentenced to life under three-strikes laws throughout the country, credited Trump for picking up the "mantle" initiated under the Obama administration for the "accelerated reform of federal sentencing laws by championing the First Step Act," noting that "the number of people in federal prison has grown during the Biden administration."

He urged Biden, therefore, to champion the implementation of "a little-used law that allows prison officials to recommend to federal judges that they reevaluate sentences of people for 'extraordinary and compelling reasons.'" This would "include people who are facing long sentences and have already served many years behind bars, have shown their commitment to rehabilitation and are prepared for release."[6] As we will see, this is an intricate part of the First Step Act.

The viability and implementation of the First Step Act and sentencing reform looms, therefore, as part of the national presidential debates on how our country can effectively tackle our mass incarceration problem.

* * *

With the president's support, the First Step Act resoundingly passed the House by a vote of 360–59 and the Senate by 87–12, making it a huge bipartisan piece of legislation. This was remarkable for a Congress that was so politically polarized at that time—and still is. No other piece of major legislation that year came close to such bipartisan support. Democratic senator Richard Durbin of Illinois, who led the push in the Senate for passage of the bill, together with Republican senators Charles Grassley of Iowa and Mike Lee of Utah, commented, "I can't remember any bill that has this kind of support, left and right, liberal and conservative, Democrat and Republican."[7]

Credit Jared Kushner, President Trump's son-in-law. He was a passionate proponent of sentencing reform, and, if not for him, there probably would be no First Step Act. He worked tirelessly to create the statute and to use his influence with his father-in-law and his Republican Party to secure its passage. He spent months quietly pressing the president to prioritize criminal justice reform policies, carving out time in his father-in-law's schedule for meetings on the topic, including a visit to the Oval Office by West and Kardashian. He personally rallied key Republican and Democratic lawmakers to support the bill, which he pitched to the president as a rare bipartisan deal and persuaded Senate Republican majority leader Mitch McConnell to bring to a vote.

But why? Was it because of Kushner's religious faith as an orthodox Jew and the Bible's embrace of redemption? It probably was more personal.

When Kushner was in his early twenties and a college student, his father, Charles Kushner, pled guilty to eighteen criminal counts, including tax evasion and witness tampering. He was sentenced to two years in prison—the most he could receive under a plea deal with Chris Christie, who was then the New Jersey U.S. attorney.

Christie characterized it as "one of the most loathsome disgusting crimes" he ever prosecuted.[8]

The elder Kushner's fall from grace happened after "he hatched a scheme for revenge and intimidation" against his sister's husband when he learned his brother-in-law was cooperating with the feds' investigation into Charles' tax evasion crimes. "Kushner hired a prostitute to lure his brother-in-law, then arranged to have the encounter in a New Jersey motel room recorded with a hidden camera and the recording sent to his own sister, the man's wife."[9]

To his credit, Jared's father acknowledged and repented his criminal misdeeds and asked not to be pardoned. Nonetheless, his son's father-in-law did not honor his request, and the president issued the following statement when he granted Charles Kushner clemency:

> Since completing his sentence in 2006, Mr. Kushner has been devoted to important philanthropic organizations and causes, such as Saint Barnabas Medical Center and United Cerebral Palsy. This record of reform and charity overshadows Mr. Kushner's conviction and 2-year sentence for preparing false tax returns, witness retaliation, and making false statements to the FEC.[10]

Indeed, after serving his time, Charles Kushner has led an exemplary life, contributing significant sums of his wealth from his billion-dollar real estate empire to numerous charities.

The younger Kushner has talked openly about how deeply his father's imprisonment impacted his life. In his early twenties, Jared suddenly found himself having to run the family's businesses while shuttling back and forth on weekends from college to see his father in an Alabama federal jail. As he told the Associated Press,

> When you're on the other side of the system, you feel so helpless. I felt like, I was on this side of the system, so

how can I try to do whatever I can do to try to be helpful
to the people who are going through it.[10]

Whether Jared would have become a zealous leader of sentencing
reform if not for his father's incarceration is debatable. But nothing
before in his privileged life would have predicted that Jared Kushner would become the titular father of the First Step Act.

So what is the First Step Act all about?

The act is a large bill: fifty-seven pages of dense text with 618
sections divided into six titles.

The first portion focuses on the need for rehabilitation in order
to reduce our recidivism rate. Employment is the key. Without
the ability to support themselves honestly, people returning from
prison must often resort to criminal means. Thus, the three-year
recidivist rate for those employed for one year post-release is just
16%; by contrast, of those who remain unemployed, 52% will likely
be back in jail.[11]

Norway has the lowest recidivism rate. Only 20% of all individuals released from incarceration will return to jail within five years.
The Norwegian system attempts to ensure that "when the sentence
has been served, [the person] is drug-free or in control of his drug
use, has a suitable place to live, can read, write and do math, has
a chance on the job market, can relate to family and friends and
society at large, is able to seek help for problems that may arise after
release and live independently."[12]

While there is an enormous difference between the humanity
and resources with which other countries address their post-prison
population, the First Step Act recognizes the need for the United States to embrace effective rehabilitation to address our mass
incarceration problem and to rid ourselves of the embarrassing and
unenvious position of having the highest recidivism rate of any
country in the world.

After brief sections allowing federal correctional officers to carry concealed firearms on Bureau of Prison premises, and a section limiting the use of restraints on federal prisoners who are pregnant or in postpartum recovery, a section of the First Step Act on sentencing reform is more substantive. Essentially, it tweaks Congress's mandatory minimum laws, but not by much. The mandatory sentence for a high-level offense after one prior conviction is reduced from twenty to fifteen years, and from life to twenty-five years for a high-level offense after two or more prior convictions. In addition, it allows courts to impose a sentence below the mandatory minimum for certain nonviolent, cooperative drug defendants with a limited criminal history, and it reduces from twenty-five to fifteen years the enhanced mandatory minimum prison term for a defendant who uses a firearm in a crime of violence or drug offense after a prior conviction for such offense. Finally, it makes the Fair Sentencing Act of 2010 retroactive. That statute reduced the severe sentences for crack cocaine convictions, which were disproportionally more punitive than non–crack cocaine crimes.

Over two hundred years ago, when the first Crimes Act became law in 1790, Congress created twenty-three federal crimes, seven of which carried mandatory minimums—always death. The rest had only statutory maximums. The death penalty was imposed for treason, murder, three piracy offenses, rescue of a person convicted of a capital crime, and, curiously, forgery of a U.S. public security. Between that time and the Civil War era, Congress started to impose mandatory minimums for a range of noncapital cases for crimes ranging from manslaughter to horse stealing to bigamy. By the 1870s, at least 108 crimes had mandatory punishments, half of which were about income taxes. But when Congress enacted the Criminal Code in 1909, 31 of these were repealed.

Except for some alcohol-related offenses during Prohibition,

Congress was quiet on the topic of mandatory minimums during the first half of the twentieth century. Then, in the latter half, things really started to heat up. With the Omnibus Crime Control Act of 1970, Congress established a mandatory minimum for using a firearm during the commission of a felony, and with the Protection of Children Against Sexual Exploitation Act of 1977, the first mandatory minimum for child pornography came into existence. This marked the beginning of a spate of congressional acts establishing mandatory minimums for a whole range of child pornography and sexual abuse cases, leading to the passage of the Adam Walsh Child Protection and Safety Act of 2006, which mandated long periods of incarceration for both receivers and creators of child pornography. During the 1980s, Congress focused on drug offenses with the Anti-Drug Abuse Acts of 1986 and 1988.

The upshot of this mandatory minimum feeding frenzy was that by 2010, four basic categories of crimes had caught the mandatory minimum attention of Congress: Drug trafficking led the pack with 66.7% of such crimes carrying minimums, pornography/prostitution (54.2%), sexual abuse (34.7%), and firearms (30.6%).[13]

There is no doubt that Congress had the right to create such sentencing mandates. As the Supreme Court stated in *Chapman v. United States*: "Congress has the power to define criminal punishments without giving the courts any sentencing discretion."[14] In *Ewing v. California*, the high court noted that the only limit to the exercise of that power is the Eighth Amendment's prohibition against cruel and inhuman treatment, which contains a "narrow proportionality principle" for noncapital sentences. But the court explained that "successful challenges to the proportionality of particular sentences have been extremely rare." Thus, it would come into play only in extreme cases—for example, "if a legislature made overtime parking a felony punishable by life imprisonment"—but not, as in *Ewing*, when it imposed a sentence of twenty-five to life for a defendant convicted of his third felony, even though that felony was for stealing three golf clubs.[15]

Whether a defendant in a federal case will be charged with a crime carrying a mandatory minimum is a decision made by the U.S. Attorney's Office of each of the country's ninety-four judicial districts in the exercise of its prosecutorial discretion. These districts roughly track the population of each state. Thus, New York is divided into four districts. I sit in the Eastern District, which, as I previously wrote, covers three of New York City's five boroughs—Brooklyn, Queens, and Staten Island—plus the two counties of Long Island: Nassau and Suffolk. The Southern District covers the other two boroughs—Manhattan and the Bronx—plus Westchester County and several other counties near Manhattan. The Northern District covers Albany and the central part of the state, and the Western District covers Buffalo and the western counties. Some states with small populations have just one judicial district, and North and South Dakota share one.

The exercise of the U.S. attorney's prosecutorial discretion in a particular district is invariably affected by the sociocultural and political climate of the district. For example, in 2010, seven of the country's ninety-four districts accounted for 27% of cases involving convictions with a mandatory penalty: the Southern and Western Districts of Texas, the Southern and Middle Districts of Florida, the Southern District of California, and the Districts of Arizona and South Carolina.

I am no fan of congressionally imposed mandatory sentences. Presently 20% of all crimes created by Congress carry mandatory minimums. While the Constitution created three branches of government, it would be foolish to believe that they are each independent. Congress has a stranglehold over the judicial branch. Congress creates the judiciary's budget, fixes the number of its judges and their salaries, creates the crimes that are to be prosecuted, and fixes the nature and extent of sentences. Thus, Congress could require more than 20% of its crimes to carry mandatory minimums. Theoretically, it could create mandatory minimums for *every* federal crime. The upshot is that the sentencing discretion of the district judge is totally controlled by Congress's wishes.

It will come as no surprise that I, and many of my sentencing colleagues, are opposed to congressionally imposed mandatory minimums. They deprive us of any discretion and are a tool of the legislative branch of government, which is more responsive to politics than to the fair application of the law based on each defendant's personal characteristics, such as whether the crime was aberrational for an otherwise law-abiding citizen or, on the other hand, a pattern of criminal activity.

Thus, I had to impose a fifteen-year sentence on an army vet who was decorated for fighting for our country in Afghanistan and Iraq and was then a respected New York City police officer. His crime was using the internet for soliciting nude photographs from teenagers he never met. Nor did he know their ages. One of them, for example, was seventeen, one year below the age of consent. When I sentenced him, I told him that Congress—not I—was sentencing him since I was just the messenger and had no choice. While some punishment was required, the fifteen years was clearly overly harsh and, in my opinion, totally inappropriate. If my hands were not tied, I thought that five years would be a far more appropriate and fairer sentence.

On the other hand, I have sentenced a despicable child pornographer who preyed on many little children to more than the fifteen-year minimum, and I have sentenced an international sex trafficker to fifty years.

In short, it should be the judge—not Congress—who imposes the sentence. The judge is trained in the law and has the responsibility to impose a fair sentence based on a balancing of the crime with the uniqueness of each individual, rather than on a politically motivated one-size-fits-all blanket sentence.

The next part of the First Step Act authorizes some new educational programs in prisons, jails, and juvenile facilities but repeals funding for drug treatment alternatives to incarceration. This was hardly a rehabilitation-reform measure and was apparently perceived by the congressional reformers as politically necessary to assuage those who were not inclined to embrace the act. For several years, my district has pioneered, with resounding success, drug-related programs to facilitate diversion and rehabilitation for those hooked on drugs.

Other sections offer a litany of reforms: they establish partnerships between prisons and faith- or community-based nonprofit organizations, make feminine hygiene products available free of charge, require that incarceration take place within five hundred miles of the incarcerated person's primary residence, encourage home confinement for low-risk offenders, modify eligibility for an elderly offender early-release pilot program, require the Bureau of Prisons to help individuals being released to obtain documents such as Social Security cards and driver's licenses, and require the bureau to incorporate de-escalation procedures into its training programs.

The act also requires the Bureau of Prisons to report on its capacity to treat heroin and opioid abuse, to establish pilot programs on youth mentorship, and to collect more data. Importantly, the act prohibits juvenile solitary confinement, except as a temporary response to behavior that poses a serious and immediate risk of harm.

Although it is curiously absent from the government's summary of the First Step Act, section 603 gives me the power to reduce a prisoner's sentence and even let lifers out of jail.[16] This power comes under the heading "Increasing the Use and Transparency of Compassionate Release." Formerly, beginning in 1984 with the passage of the Comprehensive Crime Control Act, only the Bureau of Prisons could make a compassionate release motion to the district court on behalf of a defendant. The district court judge could then decide to modify the previously imposed sentence if it agreed with the bureau that "extraordinary and compelling" reasons existed. But the bureau rarely brought compassionate release motions.

The First Step Act marked a sea change in the role of the sentencing judge because, if a defendant has not been successful in the defendant's application to the Bureau of Prisons, the act now allows the defendant to apply *directly* to the district court. In other words, the defendant no longer must depend on the Bureau of Prisons to be considered for compassionate release.

This changed everything. Before the First Step Act, the Bureau of Prisons was not terribly interested in seeking sentencing reductions. For the more than thirty years when it had the sole power to do that, the number of defendants receiving relief averaged only two dozen per year, and for the most part they were cases involving inmates who were expected to die within a year or were profoundly and irremediably incapacitated. In effect, the Bureau of Prisons is now essentially irrelevant; the power to give an incarcerated person a second chance is firmly placed with the country's district court judges.

Under the First Step Act, in order to release someone who is incarcerated, the district judge must first determine that there exist "extraordinary and compelling" circumstances. If the answer is yes, the judge must then consider and balance a series of factors, commonly referred to as §3553(a) factors: the nature and circumstances of the offense; the history and characteristics of the defendant; the need for the sentence imposed to reflect the seriousness of the offense, to promote respect for the law, and to provide just punishment; the need to deter criminal conduct; the need to protect the public from the defendant; the need to provide the defendant with necessary rehabilitation; and the need to avoid unwarranted sentencing disparities.

Nowhere in the prior 1984 statute or in the First Step Act, however, has Congress identified what constitute "extraordinary and compelling" circumstances. However, in 1984, when Congress created the U.S. Sentencing Commission, in addition to establishing the grid system, it authorized the commission to create guidelines ascribing "extraordinary and compelling" reasons for a sentence reduction. The only limitation was that rehabilitation alone could not be such a reason.

Nonetheless, as Professor William W. Berry III explains, while Congress required the Sentencing Commission to identify the extraordinary and compelling reasons for sentence reduction, "prior to 2007, [the commission] provided no guidance to the Bureau of Prisons as to what it believed constituted an 'extraordinary and compelling' circumstance."[17] The Bureau of Prisons used its exclusive power to bring motions for compassionate relief "sparingly," which Professor Berry ascribed, in part, to the "lack of a guiding standard."[18]

In 2007, however, the Sentencing Commission introduced guidelines defining three extraordinary and compelling circumstances: a defendant is suffering from a terminal illness, a defendant is experiencing significant decline related to the aging process that makes it impossible to care for him- or herself within a prison, or the defendant's only family member capable of caring for the defendant's minor child has died or become incapacitated.[19]

The 2007 guideline amendment also introduced what has come to be known as the catchall clause. It provided that the Bureau of Prisons can determine "extraordinary and compelling reasons other than, or, in combination with" reasons described elsewhere in the guidelines.[20]

In 2016, the Sentencing Commission added "an age-based category" for compassionate release eligibility, which would apply if the defendant is "at least 65 years old, is experiencing a serious deterioration in health because of the aging process, and has served at least ten years or 75% of his or her term of imprisonment (whichever is less)."[21]

By 2018, the Sentencing Commission had expanded its definition of "extraordinary and compelling circumstances" to include reasons that "need not have been unforeseen at the time of sentence in order to warrant a reduction in the term of imprisonment."[22]

This was the law when the First Step Act was enacted in 2018, and even though it technically still reads that the Bureau of Prisons makes the extraordinary and compelling determination, most of the country's thirteen circuit courts, including the Second Circuit Court of Appeals, have now ruled that the First Step Act has "freed district courts to exercise their discretion in determining what are extraordinary circumstances."[23]

I am a creature of the Second Circuit and am bound to follow the law of my circuit court of appeals. Each circuit court sits in three-judge panels to hear appeals from the decisions of the district courts in its circuit. The Second Circuit hears appeals from the district courts of New York, Connecticut, and Vermont.

The district courts are the first tier of the federal judicial pecking order. They are the trial courts and the courts of general jurisdiction. Their judges preside over all civil and criminal trials and handle all civil and criminal motions. And they are the ones who sentence convicted defendants.

About 98% of all federal cases begin and end at the district courts. It is not 100% because, if you do not like the district judge's decision, you can try to get the judge reversed by the circuit's court of appeals. And if you do not like the appeal court's decision, you can try to get the Supreme Court to take your case. That's a real longshot, though, because the high court hears fewer than one hundred cases a year. Many of those cases entail circuit splits since not all circuit courts are on the same page, and the Supreme Court must decide which circuit court to follow.

Unfortunately, most of the circuit courts have yet to embrace the full sweep of the profound changes wrought by the First Step Act. In general, circuit court judges, in reviewing district court decisions, have restricted relief for those at high risk under COVID-19. A February 2023 report to the Sentencing Commission by Professor Erica Zunkel, of the University of Chicago Law School's Criminal and Juvenile Justice Clinic, calculated that since the peak of the COVID-19 pandemic, the Bureau of Prisons filed a compassionate release motion in just 1.2% of cases, and judges granted just over 25% of these—"70% of which were for COVID-19."[24]

The report recognized, however, that "many judges have embraced their discretion to grant compassionate release for a variety of extraordinary and compelling reasons, including extreme sentencing disparities, draconian sentences, nonretroactive sentencing changes, problematic government charging decisions, and sexual abuse in prison." But it concluded that, because judges have rarely encountered compassionate release motions in the past, due to the Bureau of Prisons' unwillingness to submit them, many district judges believe that compassionate release is "primarily for medical circumstances" and are "reticent to exercise their discretion to recognize that their discretion can—and does—go further."

So what is the law of my Second Circuit governing compassionate release motions? It's spelled out in a 2020 decision in a case named

United States v. Brooker.[25] Well before that decision, the Supreme Court had ruled in 2005, in a landmark case called *United States v. Booker* (not to be confused with *Brooker*) that the district judges should consider the Sentencing Commission's guidelines, but they were simply advisory and could not preclude the judges from exercising their sound sentencing discretion.[26] Significantly, the Second Circuit, in *Brooker*, stated that when considering whether to revisit an initial sentence under the First Step Act, "a district court's discretion in this area—as in all sentencing matters—is broad."[27]

But what are the factors that I and all the other district judges throughout the country can or should consider under the undefined catchall clause?

Brooker concludes that it's appropriate to consider a defendant's extensive rehabilitation while in prison, coupled with the length of the sentence, in assessing whether the requisite "extraordinary and compelling" bar has been met, and adds that "these arguments may also interact with the present coronavirus pandemic, which courts around the country, including in this district, have used as justification for granting some sentence reductions."

Notwithstanding these comments, the country's district courts have not been provided with any consistent guidance from their circuit courts as to the breadth of their discretion, and there certainly is no uniformity among all the circuit courts about what they may consider under the catchall clause. So the law is developing on a case-by-case basis, and it certainly is the subject of intense debate.

Although I wish the *Brooker* court had provided more guidance, I like the Second Circuit's forward-minded comment in that case that I have "broad" discretion in crafting what I believe should be the factors I should consider in making my "extraordinary and compelling" determinations. But I was particularly struck by the court's comment that this discretion was the same "as in all sentencing matters." The public has little appreciation of just how broad this discretion can be. As I read this comment in *Brooker* it reminded me of the *Fitch* case, because it was a stark example of the extraordinary power of the sentencing judge—and, by contrast, the relatively minor role of the jury.

The case came to me as I was randomly assigned to sit as a designated court of appeals judge for the Ninth Circuit. For the past seventeen years I had sat as a visiting designated circuit judge for that appellate court to help it cut its huge backlog of appeals. Even though I have always been a district judge from New York, I'm allowed to sit as an ersatz circuit judge if asked to help.

Circuit courts sit in three-judge panels, two of which must be from the circuit. On the *Fitch* panel, in addition to myself, were Ninth Circuit judges Randy Smith and Alfred Goodwin. The Ninth Circuit is the largest circuit. Its court of appeals hears appeals from the district courts of nine states: Alaska, Arizona, California, Hawaii, Idaho, Montana, Nevada, Oregon, and Washington, as well as Guam. Because it is so large, it has four courthouses, in Seattle, Portland, San Francisco, and Pasadena. Appeals from Nevada go to San Francisco, where I was assigned to sit.

David Fitch had been indicted and convicted after a jury trial for several garden-variety, low-level crimes related to the fraudulent use of the credit card and bank account of his wife, Maria Bozi, who had mysteriously disappeared. The typical sentence for these types of crimes is a couple of years. But Judge James Mahan, a Nevada district judge who presided over the trial, sentenced Fitch to 262 months—just shy of twenty-two years—because he decided that Fitch must have killed his wife. The judge did this even though Fitch was neither convicted nor even indicted and tried for murdering her. And for all we know she might even be alive.

I had to decide—together with the two Ninth Circuit appellate judges—whether the law permitted Judge Mahan to sentence Fitch for a crime he was never charged with committing, let alone one for murder.

But what about the jurors? They have nothing to do with sentencing except in a few situations. Once they decide that a defendant is guilty, it is the district judge who has the sole power to determine the facts and circumstances that will drive the sentence. The *Fitch* case is a poignant example of just how expansive that power is.

In sentencing Fitch to about twenty-two years—even though the sentencing range for the crimes for which he was convicted was under five years—Judge Mahan believed that an upward departure was warranted because he determined that the death of Fitch's wife "was the means that Mr. Fitch used to effectuate the offenses of which he was found guilty." That issue was never before the jury. But once the jury found Fitch guilty of bank fraud, Judge Mahan had the power to decide that Fitch killed his wife and to sentence him accordingly. That was because the Supreme Court ruled years ago that the sentencing judge may consider facts that a jury may not—and the judge may even find those facts by a lesser standard than proof beyond a reasonable doubt.

Thus, the judge can increase the defendant's sentence based—as in Fitch's case—on uncharged conduct (and even for *acquitted* conduct). In coming to this seemingly counterintuitive conclusion, the high court reasoned that such increases "do not punish a defendant for crimes of which he was not convicted, but rather increase his sentence because of the manner in which he committed the crime of conviction."[28]

Except where Congress has established mandatory minimum punishments, the sentencing judge's power is still the case today. The only constitutional limitation on this enormous power is that Judge Mahan, for example, could not sentence Fitch beyond the maximums that Congress had established for the crimes for which he was convicted. They included, in addition to the bank fraud, a variety of other relatively minor crimes, such as fraudulent use of an access device and money laundering. Collectively, these other crimes also carried high maximums. When stacked together, which the sentencing court could do, the total maximum range came to an astonishing 360 years. This was the outer limit of Judge Mahan's sentencing authority. The practical upshot of it all was that Fitch's fate—once convicted of the minor crimes—was totally in the hands of the judge.

Of course, there had to be a factual basis for the judge's determination that Fitch had indeed murdered his wife to carry out his bank fraud and credit card crimes. And in fixing the precise sentence, the judge had to consider the individual characteristics of the defendant. But even there, Judge Mahan had boundless discretion. He could obtain information on which to make his findings and fix the term of imprisonment from any reliable source, such as the presentence report prepared by the Probation Department, which draws on information concerning every aspect of a defendant's life. Justice Hugo Black explained the rationale for this when he wrote the majority opinion for the Supreme Court in 1949 in *Williams v. People of the State of New York*:

> A sentencing judge . . . is not confined to the narrow issue of guilt. His task within fixed statutory or constitutional limits is to determine the type and extent of punishment after the issue of guilt has been determined. And modern concepts of individualizing punishment have made it all the more necessary that a sentencing judge not be denied an opportunity to obtain pertinent information by a requirement of rigid adherence to restrictive rules of evidence properly applicable to the trial.[29]

The *Williams* case stands as a stark example of the power of a sentencing judge even to override a jury's determination. There, a New York State jury found the defendant guilty of murder in the first degree—which then qualified for the imposition of the death penalty—but unanimously recommended a life sentence. Relying on the additional information that the trial judge obtained through the court's Probation Department, the judge sentenced Williams to death. The high court approved by a 7–2 vote, thereby setting a precedent for allowing a sentencing judge to consider information not before the jury in deciding whether a defendant should be executed. Justice Murphy's dissenting opinion cogently articulated the opposite view:

> I agree with the Court as to the value and humaneness of liberal use of probation reports as developed by modern penologists, but, in a capital case, against the unanimous recommendation of a jury, where the report would concededly not have been admissible at the trial, and was not subject to examination by the defendant, I am forced to conclude that the high commands of due process were not obeyed.

I personally agree with Justice Murphy's dissent, but it remains to this day the minority view of the Supreme Court. Its decision in *Williams* regrettably paved the way for a small number of states—only Alabama, Florida, Delaware, and Indiana—to adopt legislation to allow a trial judge to override a jury's recommendation against the death penalty, although all states abandoned the practice by 2017.[30] However, as of 2022, thirty-five people "sentenced to death via judicial override remain on death row awaiting execution."[31] But nobody in Delaware is on death row because of override, and it has been fifteen years since a Florida judge has exercised override to impose the ultimate penalty. Not so in Alabama. A searing 2014 *New Yorker* article by Paige Williams reported that

> [i]n thirty-one of the past thirty-two years, Alabama's judges have condemned someone to death through override at least once. . . . Nearly seventy Alabama judges have single-handedly ordered an inmate's execution, and collectively they have done so more than a hundred times. Thirty-six of the nearly two hundred convicts on death row are there because of override.[32]

Fortunately, there is no *federal* law that allows a federal judge to override a jury's verdict against the imposition of the death penalty in the statutes where Congress has put the death penalty in play—such as murder in aid of racketeering and terrorism-related murders. But, as in *Fitch*, so long as the sentencing judge does not exceed the high maximum sentences that Congress has fixed, the judge's sentencing discretion is enormous.

Judge Mahan made six specific findings to support his conclusion that "Mr. Fitch caused Maria Bozi's death" and that "the cause of death of Bozi was the means that Mr. Fitch used to effectuate the offenses of which he was found guilty": (1) he failed to report her disappearance to the police; (2) he told different stories to different people about her whereabouts; (3) he tried to sell her clothing and personal effects; (4) he remarried shortly after her disappearance without first seeking a divorce; (5) he had possession of her checkbook, credit cards, and other personal information that any person would have on their person; and (6) he raided her bank account and credit cards by either disguises or forgeries. The judge believed these findings were supported by clear and convincing evidence from the trial testimony and undisputed facts contained in the Probation Department's presentence report.[33]

The judge then settled on a fifteen-level upward departure, which upped the sentencing range from 41 to 51 months to 210 to 262 months and sentenced Fitch to the upper limit. Fitch appealed. Because his case came from the Nevada federal district court, his appeal would be before a panel of three judges for the Ninth Circuit Court of Appeals.

Unless the judges decide that an appeal is of little merit and can be summarily disposed of on the briefs, the lawyers are given the opportunity to appear before the panel for oral argument. Based on the perceived complexity of the case by the clerk's office, both sides are usually given between 10 and 20 minutes to make their points. The lawyers are invariably questioned by the judges to get to the heart of the issues.

The *Fitch* appeal was obviously one that merited oral argument, and I jumped at the opportunity to question the government's lawyer, Gregory Damm, as to why Fitch was not prosecuted for murder. His responses were illuminating.

MR. DAMM: I always hoped that we would find Maria Bozi's body to put some closure to this case. But as you well know, in the federal government we have a limited jurisdiction to charge violent crimes, in this case murder. We don't know exactly where Mr. Fitch disposed of Maria Bozi's body. We had some belief that he rented a boat and dumped her body in Lake Mead. We had some belief that he went to the Grand Canyon to some remote area. . . .

JUDGE BLOCK: You don't need the body to bring a murder charge against him.

MR. DAMM: No, but you need venue, and we didn't have

venue. We don't know that she was murdered on a federal enclave.

JUDGE BLOCK: What comes out in the wash is that you couldn't get him for murder directly, so in effect you got him indirectly for murder, right?

MR. DAMM: We certainly did.

Damm was probably right about the lack of federal venue, but I wondered why Fitch could not have been prosecuted before a jury for murder in the Nevada state court. Upon reflection, I should have asked him that question out of curiosity, but it really made no difference. Under the law, the government had the power to prosecute Fitch in federal court for the bank and credit card frauds—which are federal crimes. It did not have to run the risk of a state court jury finding Fitch innocent of murder. It could simply leave it up to the sentencing judge in the federal case to sentence him "indirectly."

I listened to a few other oral arguments that day, but none were as dramatic or as interesting as the *Fitch* case. Afterward, I met with the other two panel judges to discuss the cases. We voted on each one and decided whether any of them merited a lengthy, full-blown written opinion or whether they could be disposed of in a short memorandum. We believed that *Fitch* warranted a comprehensive written opinion, and I was assigned the task of writing it.

I started my opinion by commenting that "[b]ecause Fitch has never been charged with his wife's murder, his sentence is a poignant example of a drastic upward departure from the guidelines range—albeit below the statutory maximum—based on uncharged criminal conduct." Nonetheless, even though I recognized that the court "had not had occasion to address a scenario quite like this," I believed that under the law, we were "constrained" to uphold Judge Mahan's decision.

My opinion then tracked the key decisions of the Supreme Court, concluding that it "remains the law that the sentencing judge has the power to sentence a defendant based upon facts not found by a jury up to the statutory maximum, and that 'the defendant has no right to a jury determination of the facts that the judge deems relevant.'" I explained that the only restrictions on a district court's power to impose a sentence—provided it is less than the statutory maximum—are "that the sentence must not be tainted by procedural error, and that it must not be substantively unreasonable."

But my opinion did not dissuade Judge Goodwin from dissenting. He did not agree with Judge Smith and me that there was clear and convincing evidence that Fitch murdered his wife because "[w]e simply do not know any of the circumstances of Bozi's disappearance." Of course, I thought that my opinion effectively explained why we had to affirm Judge Mahan's decision, and I suspect that Judge Goodwin just wasn't comfortable with acknowledging the harshness of the law that allows a single human being—although a judge—to convict a person for an uncharged crime (and even by a lesser standard than proof beyond a reasonable doubt), especially one as serious as murder.[34]

I believed that Judge Mahan was perfectly competent to decide that David Fitch murdered Maria Bozi, but I did wonder—as I suspect Judge Goodwin did as well—what was left to that quaint notion of trial by jury?

There is not a criminal defense lawyer I have ever spoken to about the *Fitch* case who can comprehend how the law allows for a judge to make findings of fact—let alone not based on the criminal standard for fact finding by a jury of "proof beyond a reasonable doubt"—and to sentence a defendant to jail based on uncharged conduct. I never believed that I had that power until the *Fitch* case. But their disbelief is even more startling when I tell them that I even have the power to impose a sentence based on acquitted conduct.

Just a few months after *Fitch*, I had to decide whether I could sentence a young man to life who had been convicted for drug crimes and carrying a gun but acquitted of murder. I started the sentencing proceeding by announcing that under the law, the judge—not the jury—has the responsibility to take into consideration, in fixing the sentence, uncharged conduct (as in *Fitch*) and even acquitted conduct, as in this case. This was now the moment when I had to decide whether to hold an acquitted defendant responsible for murder.

The government argued that the evidence clearly justified finding that the defendant had murdered the victim, and the Probation Department's presentence report recommended that—notwithstanding the jury's acquittal—I make the requisite murder finding and sentence the defendant to 420 months (thirty-five years). Under the law, five years was mandatory because of the conviction for carrying a gun. The other thirty years was the maximum that Congress had created for the drug crimes, which gave me—just like Judge Mahan in *Fitch*—enormous sentencing discretion.

I decided not to do it. But it was not an easy decision. There was plenty of evidence that could easily have supported the decision to impose a sentence corresponding to a murder conviction, and, as I commented: "I'm terribly concerned that there's a dead boy here and . . . there's a lot about what I heard that makes me believe that [the defendant] was the killer." Ultimately, however, I reasoned that, unlike *Fitch*, the case turned on the credibility of the witnesses. In my mind, that was the big difference. Added to the mix was my intuitive discomfort with countermanding a jury's verdict.

When I tell regular folks that I can put someone in jail for life based on uncharged criminal conduct, let alone acquitted conduct, they think I must be drinking too much. But such is the law and it reinforces the fact that—other than mandatory minimums—I have enormous sentencing discretion, especially since the Sentencing Commission's guidelines are only advisory.

The *Brooker* case also means that my resentencing discretion with respect to compassionate release under the First Step Act is "broad." The only restriction is that my decision may not be based solely on rehabilitation. Not all circuit courts have embraced the *Brooker* court's "broad" reach and its analogy to "all sentencing." The breadth of the sentencing judge's discretion throughout the country in deciding when a prisoner is entitled to a second chance is a hot-button item and may ultimately be determined by the Supreme Court in the absence of congressional interdiction. But for me, when deciding whether to give Volpe, Birkett, Smith, Russo, Amuso, and Casso a second chance, "broad" sentencing discretion was foremost in my mind.

On April 27, 2023, shortly after Professor Zunkel filed her report with the newly constituted Sentencing Commission, the commission enacted new proposed advisory guidelines. They became effective on November 1, 2023, and in the main track the circuit court's decision in *Brooker*.

Importantly, the commission retained the catchall "other reasons" category, recognizing that it could not possibly identify the myriad extraordinary and compelling reasons that might warrant a sentence reduction. It recognized that "during the period between the enactment of the First Step Act in 2018 and this amendment, district courts around the country based sentence reductions on dozens of reasons and a combination of reasons." Based on "a careful review of those cases," the Commission believed that judges are "in a unique position to determine whether the circumstances warrant a reduction." Therefore, it reasoned that ultimately "what circumstances or combination of circumstances are sufficiently extraordinary and compelling to warrant a reduction in sentence is best provided by reviewing courts, rather than through an effort by the commission to predict and specify in advance all of the grounds on which relief may be appropriate."[35]

I have had many compassionate release motions for sentence reductions since the advent of the First Step Act. The six that I have picked for this book identify several factors that weighed heavily in my decisions. I am sure that not all my colleagues will agree with each of my decisions—nor probably will you. But they raise the profound issue of when, if at all, a defendant is now entitled to a second chance.

What follows is how I applied these factors and decided the compassionate release motions to the six representative cases I wrote about in part I.

PART III
THE SENTENCES

8

JUSTIN VOLPE

Justin Volpe filed his compassionate release motion two days before Christmas 2020. He filed pro se, using a form supplied by the Bureau of Prisons, meaning he had no lawyer at that time. In his own handwriting, he wrote that his term of imprisonment was 360 months, that he had served approximately twenty-one years, six months (258 months), and that his projected release date was January 9, 2025. He was then forty-eight.

Volpe checked off a box where he reported that the warden had denied his request for compassionate release; therefore, he had exhausted his administrative remedy. He then checked off a series of other boxes: that he was not "70 years old or older"; that he had not "served 30 years or more of imprisonment" for "the offense or offenses for which you are imprisoned"; and that "the Director of Prisons determined that you are not a danger to the safety of any other person or the community."[1] In that respect he inserted "'PATTERN' RISK SCORE = MINIMUM." He then checked "yes" in answer to the question of whether "you believe there are other extraordinary and compelling reasons for your release" and gave a handwritten explanation:

> There is a widespread Covid-19 outbreak currently at Beaumont-Low despite the institution's efforts and claims. On Nov. 06, 2020, I tested positive for Covid-19 and had several symptoms. No medical treatment of any kind was provided or offered. There is no conclusive medical evidence on the long-term effects of this virus. Please let me have the chance to meet any needs with private insurance and at home with my family's love. It is impossible to social/physical distance in tight open-dorms, bunk beds are less than 3 feet apart. Toilets, showers, sinks are constantly broken. Mold is prevalent.

Last, he checked a box requesting that "an attorney be appointed to help me."

Volpe also added an attachment setting forth "Additional Compelling Reasons." In it he wrote,

> In 1997, I committed a serious wrong and crime. I take full responsibility and live with the pain it has caused the victim, his family, and others. For over two decades I have tried to live in a way to make up for it, including completing over 145 classes, from, 3 vocational trainings, one 4-year HVAC apprenticeship, victim impact, anger management and spiritual growth course.
>
> If sentenced in 2020, there is the chance a judge could be allowed to issue a lower sentence due to "Guidelines" not being mandatory and absolute anymore.
>
> I do not seek to evade just punishment for my crime. I have served the overwhelming majority of my sen-

tence. After 21 plus years in prison, it is my family who is being punished more. I respectfully ask for your consideration to have the ability to help my dear 76-year-old mother (Grace) who is a widow and needs physical and emotional help, as well as my loyal wife (Caroline) who meets all the demands of a household all on her own during these trying and uncertain times.

Thank you for taking the time to consider these and other unspoken, heartfelt reasons.

Sincerely,
Justin Volpe

* * *

On February 1, 2021, the government opposed Volpe's motion in a single-spaced, eleven-page email letter. The primary reason given was that the defendant "does not fall within the population of those who are most vulnerable to suffer severe consequences upon contracting COVID-19 and the defendant has himself already recovered from a relatively mild case of COVID-19."

The letter was extremely well written by Assistant U.S. Attorney Elizabeth Geddes, who happened to be one of my law clerks before she became an AUSA fifteen years ago. She had since secured convictions in major federal prosecutions. In 2011 she had helped to prosecute a large federal organized crime case, and the following year her case against the Colombo crime family resulted in thirty-eight defendants copping pleas.

Geddes had received many awards for her outstanding work. In 2013, the New York City Bar Association awarded her the Henry L. Stimson Medal for outstanding prosecutions. In 2015, the National Association of Former United States Attorneys awarded her the J. Michael Bradford Memorial Award. In 2019, the New York County Lawyers Association awarded Geddes its Public

Service Award. In 2022, the New York office of the Department of Homeland Security named Liz the "Prosecutor of the Year."

After arguing against Volpe's compassionate release, in 2022 she successfully prosecuted R & B musician Robert Sylvester Kelly, better known as R. Kelly. He was convicted after a six-week trial of racketeering and related offenses and sentenced to jail for thirty years. It was the first time Kelly was held criminally accountable for his conduct after decades of his "sexcapades." Geddes was then chief of the civil rights section of the office's criminal division.

Liz and I did not talk about her Volpe letter, but true to her tough-on-crime reputation she held no grief for him.

In the letter, Geddes took a hardline interpretation of the First Step Act, aligning herself with the restrictive view of two of the circuit courts. Notably, neither she nor Volpe in his pro se submission mentioned the Second Circuit's decision in *Brooker*.

Geddes's letter was comprehensive and persuasive. She debunked Volpe's COVID-19 argument, noting that Volpe was then forty-eight years old "and has not suffered from any serious medical issues." She wrote that "[a]s many courts have held, a generalized risk of potential exposure to COVID-19 while in custody is, alone, an insufficient basis for release." Therefore, she maintained that "Volpe has not met his burden to show that there are 'extraordinary and compelling reasons' that might permit his release at this time." Nonetheless, she argued that even if an evaluation of other factors were done, "it would weigh overwhelming against Volpe's release."

Geddes relied heavily on the nature of Volpe's original criminal act, stating that "the defendant committed one of the most heinous crimes in New York City's history." She quoted Judge Nickerson's comment when he sentenced Volpe that "short of intentional murder, one cannot imagine a more barbarous misuse of power." Thus, she concluded that "[a] sentence of 30 years—and not a lesser sentence—continues to be necessary to reflect the seriousness of the offenses, to promote respect for the law and to provide just punishment and adequate deterrence."

Volpe's pro se papers paled by comparison with Geddes's comprehensive and compelling submission. The courts were essentially shut down at that time since it was the height of the pandemic, and I did not draft a full written decision. Rather, on February 8, 2021, I instructed the court's clerk to electronically file the following order:

> Defendant Justin Volpe's motion for compassionate release is denied. He does not present any extraordinary and compelling reasons based on the possibility of contracting COVID-19. In any event, reconsideration of the §3553(a) factors does not warrant a reduction of his sentence given the grave nature and circumstances of his crime.

Volpe would have to spend the remaining four years of his sentence in jail.

As things transpired, however, Volpe was granted his freedom by the Bureau of Prisons a year before his original release date. On May 13, 2023, the bureau transferred him from his prison in Minnesota to "community confinement." A bureau spokesperson explained that community confinement "means the inmate is in either home confinement or a . . . halfway house."

Volpe was sent home. "I wish everybody well that was involved with my case," he told the *New York Post* when reporters tracked him down at his family home on Staten Island. He added, "I have nothing but love in my heart for New York City and everybody in my case, especially Mr. Louima." He continued, "I wish us all peace. I just want to rebuild my life at the pace that I'm able to. God bless everyone."[2]

In retrospect, I believe I made a hasty and improvident decision. I had such a high regard for Liz Geddes that I credited what she had written, especially when compared with Volpe's pro se papers. Moreover, at the time Volpe had submitted his motion to me, on December 23, 2020, I had yet to read the *Brooker* decision, which had been handed down just a few months before. I failed to then comprehend and embrace the sweeping discretionary power I now had to revisit a previously imposed sentence. And although I should have known about *Brooker*, I was not alerted to it by either Geddes or Volpe.

I was not alone. The *Brooker* view that compassionate release motions deserved a "broad" application had not been adopted by a number of the circuit courts, as reflected by the Seventh and Third Circuit decisions cited by Geddes in her letter. And my colleagues were also slow in accepting the First Step Act's new sentencing discretion. It would take a while for it to sink in. Thus, the first spate of decisions from many of my colleagues summarily denied these motions, as I did in Volpe's case. It was not until the following year that I got up to speed and overcame my initial knee-jerk reaction that only in the rarest of cases involving severe medical conditions should a compassionate release motion be granted.

But such is how law is made.

I also wondered if I had done the right thing when I later read Abner Louima's comments on Volpe's motion. He had told the *New York Daily News*, "It's up to the justice system, it's not up to me. It's so many years after the crime. Twenty-one years is not 21 days. I think at least he's spent enough time thinking about his actions."[3]

Under the law, Volpe had no automatic right to a lawyer for post-trial proceedings, and I never granted his request for the appointment of counsel—it was entirely in my discretion. But if I had assigned Volpe a lawyer, the result might have been different.

I thought about that a few years later when I appointed counsel to represent Sherwin Birkett. It made a huge difference.

9

SHERWIN BIRKETT

I had asked one of my three very smart law clerks if I could do it. Not surprisingly, she did not find any statutory or case authority. But I reasoned that the Code of Conduct for U.S. Judges, adopted by the Judicial Conference, allowed me to appoint a lawyer to a person seeking early release. The conference was created by Congress in 1922 and consists of a series of "canons" designed to frame policy guidelines for the federal courts. It is led by the chief justice of the U.S. Supreme Court, and its membership is composed of all the circuits' chiefs and a handful of district judges whom the Supreme Court chief justice appoints. Violations of the code subjects a judge to disciplinary actions.

The commentary to the first canon, requiring a judge to "uphold the integrity and independence of the judiciary," states that "the canons are rules of reason" and "should be applied consistently with constitutional requirements, statutes, other court rules and decisional law, and in the context of all relevant circumstances."[1] I reasoned that since the concepts of justice and fairness were the bedrock principles governing the exercise of judicial power, assigning counsel to represent Birkett was, under these unique circumstances, the fair and just thing to do.

In any event, who could complain? Surely the government would not seek to reverse any favorable decision I would make for Birkett because he had a lawyer. A move like that would make it a laughingstock. Sometimes, common sense trumps adherence to a rigid judicial playbook. I subscribe to the adage: Rules are for the guidance of wise men and the obedience of fools.

Other canons provide that judges should "avoid impropriety and the appearance of impropriety in all activities"; "perform the duties of the office fairly, impartially and diligently"; and refrain from engaging in "extrajudicial activities" that are not consistent with the judge's judicial obligation and from "political activity."[2]

For some strange reason, as has been in the news of late, the justices of the U.S. Supreme Court are exempt from adhering to the code of conduct. The recent disclosure of some very questionable ethical behavior by two of the current Supreme Court justices created a public firestorm and has led to proposed congressional legislation to impose ethics rules on the high court.

This had created divisions among the Supreme Court justices. Justice Alito, in an interview published in the *Wall Street Journal* in July 2023, railed against Congress meddling in the high court's affairs. "Congress did not create the Supreme Court," he told the newspaper, and added, "No provision in the Constitution gives them the authority to regulate the Supreme Court—period."[3]

A few days later, at a judicial conference in Portland, Oregon, Justice Kagan took the opposite view: "Of course Congress can regulate various aspects of what the Supreme Court does." She explained that Congress sets the court's budget and makes changes to the court's jurisdiction and can increase or shrink the size of the court (which it has done over the years). She added, "Regardless of what Congress does, the court can do stuff." And explained, "We could decide to adopt a code of conduct of our own that either follows or decides in certain instances not to follow the standard codes of conduct."[4]

Chief Justice Roberts also joined the debate. In a public speech he gave the prior May, he agreed with Justice Alito that ethical concerns were "a job for the court, not Congress" but wanted "to assure people that [he was] committed to making certain that [they] as a court adhere to the highest standards of conduct." He added, "We are continuing to look at things we can do to give practical effect to that commitment with our status as an independent branch of government and the Constitution's separation of powers."[5]

In her remarks, Justice Kagan also acknowledged the court's concern about the matter, saying, "It's not a secret for me to say that we have been discussing this issue." And she put in a good word for her colleagues: "And it won't be a surprise to know that nine of us have a variety of views about this, as about most things. We're nine freethinking individuals."[6]

Be that as it may, I just do not understand why these "freethinking individuals" can't simply agree to adhere to the same judicial canons of ethics that all the rest of the country's federal court judges must comply with.

However, on November 13, 2023, the Supreme Court relented and released its own ethics code. But as Adam Liptak, the Supreme Court reporter for the *New York Times*, wrote the following day, "[I]t looks good on paper, experts in legal ethics said. But only on paper."

Liptak quoted a number of experts on the topic.

As explained by Amanda Frost, a law professor at the University of Virginia, "[t]he primary problem is how to give these rules teeth, especially in light of the fact that there have been repeated violations of these very rules." Liptak elaborated,

> At the heart of much of the debate over the new ethics code is which conflicts require recusal and whether justices should decide those questions for themselves. Justice Thomas, for instance, took part in cases on the 2020 election and its aftermath, even though Virginia Thomas, his wife, had participated in efforts to overturn the results.

"The new code does not say what can be done to address situations like that," said Renee Knake Jefferson, a law professor at the University of Houston. She explained, "There is no official process for an individual to file a complaint. There is not really even any clear way that we can see how justices will enforce it among themselves."

And Gabe Roth, the executive director of Fix the Court, an advocacy group that seeks more openness at the Supreme Court, questioned, "If the nine are going to release an ethics code with no enforcement mechanism and remain the only police of the nine, then how can the public trust they're going to do anything more than simply cover for one another, ethics be damned?"

In conclusion, Liptak reported, "Part of the rationale for issuing the new code, legal experts said, was to avoid congressional action," and quoted James Sample, a law professor at Hofstra University: "If we waited for the Supreme Court to voluntarily cede ethics enforcement power to others, we would have better odds waiting for Godot. Congress can and should pursue meaningful mechanisms to enforce the code."[7]

It remains to be seen whether Congress will act.

*   *   *

In appointing an attorney to represent Sherwin Birkett, I selected someone from the court's Criminal Justice Act list of private attorneys. Every district has a federal defenders office charged with representing indigent defendants, who are entitled to trial counsel. But the court retains the discretion to appoint someone from the private attorney list. In most districts, including mine, this list is composed of qualified criminal defense lawyers selected by a committee of the court. For several years I chaired my district's committee. We prided ourselves on selecting only highly qualified lawyers. They would be reasonably well compensated from public monies allocated to the defense of the indigent.

Birkett was indigent and had brought a pro se motion to represent himself in a request for early release under the First Step Act. Although he was not entitled to counsel as a matter of right, I appointed Royce Russell from the private attorney list to represent him. Russell had recently appeared before me, and I was impressed with his demeanor and his skilled representation of the indigent defendant.

I had never seen him in court before this recent appearance. In that case he had been assigned to represent the defendant by a magistrate judge, and I asked whether he was getting any other court-appointed assignments. Russell told me that he was on the private attorney list only a short time and had not been given many. I thought about that when I decided to appoint him to represent Birkett.

That they both were Black was an added reason to select Russell. While I do not believe in matching assigned counsel and defendant by race, sometimes it makes sense. The issue can cut both ways. I had excused one of the private list's finest Black lawyers, Gary Villanueva, because his racist white client refused to talk to him. Conversely, I assigned Villanueva to represent a belligerent Black defendant because he didn't want "a honkey white lawyer."

I had come to know Gary and we became good friends. I admired his capacity to relate to and effectively represent evil defendants—white or Black. He was currently representing a Latino MS-13 gang killer being prosecuted for the death penalty and had told me that he believed that even that despicable human being had some redeeming qualities.

Royce Russell did a good job. After conducting a hearing, I wrote an extensive opinion setting Birkett free in a few years. In assessing the "extraordinary and compelling" factors, I cobbled together several, including Birkett's rehabilitation since Judge Johnson's decision. He had from that time "earned his G.E.D. and completed several courses, as well as a non-residential drug program." Moreover, "for the past nine years, Birkett's record [had] been clean, and his last serious infraction occurred thirteen years ago." I added to the mix his susceptibility to COVID-19, that the law no longer mandated a life sentence, and that he faced deportation.

But I had two paramount concerns. First, the disparity between Birkett's lifetime sentence for exercising his right to trial and codefendant and organization leader Vassell's twenty-five-year sentence—the so-called trial tax. It did not seem right that a criminal defendant such as Birkett should receive such a significantly longer sentence for exercising a fundamental right than had he simply pled guilty. Studies have found that defendants who choose to go to trial face a 15–60% increase in average sentence length.

And my second concern—of equal if not greater consideration—was Birkett's age at the time he committed his crimes. Birkett had been in jail for thirty-two years, since he was nineteen years old. The papers Russell submitted on his behalf supplemented the information I had read in the presentence report. Birkett was just entering his teen years when he met neighborhood members of the Vassell Enterprise. They became his substitute family. At fourteen, he dropped out of school and was sent to Dallas by his elders in the organization, where he was "cared for by affiliated members" and provided with "food, clothes and shelter." He was also paid $500 weekly to distribute crack cocaine to street dealers. He began carrying a pocketknife and ended up participating in the murder of rival drug dealer Harold Spence with Paul Moore when Birkett was just eighteen years old. A year later, he and a co-conspirator killed another drug dealer, John Wilson.

As I wrote in my decision, Birkett "had known only a life of drug trafficking and its concomitant violence since he was nine years old," and I cited Judge Rakoff's comprehensive decision in a case he decided as a district judge for the Southern District of New York explaining why a defendant's youth merited serious consideration.[8]

If I had read an August 2023 article from the *New York Times* that my good friend Judge Raymond Dearie later sent me, I would have said much more. It told the story of Donnell Drinks, who was tried as an adult for murder when he was seventeen years old. He was sentenced to death and would "most likely have died in prison" if a "national effort" had not begun "to rethink the culpability of young people in the eyes of the law." Eventually, Drinks was granted parole after serving ten years behind bars.[9]

This new recognition of the special status of young people started in 2005 when the U.S. Supreme Court struck down the death penalty for minors in *Roper* v. *Simmons*, leaning heavily on new scientific research. As Justice Kennedy, who wrote the opinion for a bare 5–4 majority of the court, stated, "[A]ny parent knows that young people are not like adults. They are more impulsive, reckless and susceptible to persuasion."[10]

"Then came a series of breakthroughs. In 2010, [in *Graham v. Florida*], the Supreme Court abolished sentences of life without parole for minors charged with crimes other than murder. Two years later, [in *Miller v. Alabama*], the Supreme Court struck down all mandatory sentences of life without parole for juveniles. Four years later, in a case called *Montgomery v. Louisiana*, the court made that decision retroactive . . . giving more than 2,800 child lifers across the country the right to have their sentences revisited."[11]

I was struck by how our judge-made laws can be so circumstantial and by the profound consequences that flow from a single vote, as was the case in *Roper*, and for many significant issues of our time, from *Bush v. Gore*, which decided the presidency, to cases involving gay marriage, access to health care, and gun control.

I was involved in a case somewhat like that as well. When I sat as a visiting judge for the Ninth Circuit Court of Appeals, the presiding judge for the three-judge panel was always the circuit judge with the most seniority. The presiding judge's responsibility was to parcel out the cases before oral argument among the three of us for the preparation of a memorandum. This required the assigned judge to explain the case, delve into the applicable law, and recommend a disposition. The other judges did not have to agree with the recommendation and had the obligation to do their own research and come to an independent conclusion as to how the appeal should be decided. But the memorandum was a helpful research tool.

I would usually sit for two or three days once or twice a year and would hear about six appeals per day. Typically, I had to prepare a memorandum for two of the daily appeals. In the fall of 2018, presiding judge Stephen R. Reinhardt had assigned me to prepare a memorandum in the *Hawkins v. The Kroger Company* appeal that was to be argued in December. The assignment was randomly done. He did not know anything about the case at that time.

The Kroger Company is a large national food manufacturing business that makes and distributes many well-known food products, including Kroger Bread Crumbs. The marketing label conspicuously displayed on the outside of the Kroger Bread Crumbs package advertised to the consumer that the bread crumbs contain "0g Trans Fat per serving." This is of great comfort to the purchaser because trans fat can increase the risk of life-threatening diseases. That is why the World Health Organization was working to eliminate artificial trans fat from all foods globally by 2023.[12]

The back of the Kroger Bread Crumbs' label contained the nutrition facts panel. It also reported that the bread crumbs contained "0g trans fat." But this assessment was based on FDA regulations allowing the panel to make that representation if a bread crumb serving contained less than 0.5 grams of trans fat, as it did in this case. Thus, there were conflicting FDA regulations: in truth, the bread crumbs did indeed contain this dangerous artificial food additive, just not enough to breach the FDA's 0.5-gram cutoff on the nutrition facts panel.

The case, therefore, presented a paradox. Was Kroger liable for advertising on the face of its label that its bread crumbs did not contain trans fat when it did indeed contain trans fat, just not at a level that would require Kroger to report that fact on the nutrition panel on the reverse side of the label?

One of my law clerks drafted an extensive memorandum for my review before I would submit it to my two colleagues. After thoroughly digging into the law, he recommended that we reverse the district court's decision that was in favor of the Kroger Company. I scratched my head as I read it and said to myself, "This is terribly confusing, but I think he is right."

The memorandum thoroughly explained the origins of these inconsistent labels and the confusion caused by dense, dueling FDA regulations. My law clerk recommended that the court hold that, since the large outside label stated that the product did not contain trans fat, "a consumer reading the label in this case could be misled" into believing "that the product was free of trans fat."

He reasoned that "a requirement to state certain facts in the nutrition label is not a license to make that statement elsewhere in the product" if those facts were untrue. I agreed with the memorandum and sent it to the other two judges.

I thought this was an important case and an extensive opinion was warranted to serve a death blow to trans fat consumption in the United States since, as stated in the memorandum, "it has become increasingly recognized as a dangerous substance and a leading cause of numerous serious ailments, including heart disease and diabetes."

But when we conferenced the case after oral argument, I was surprised that Judge Reinhardt disagreed. He took a literal approach and thought that we were bound by the fact that, under the 0.5-gram FDA regulation, the nutrition panel correctly reported that the product contained zero trans fat. He said that he would write a decision to that effect and vote to affirm the district court. I tried my best to dissuade him, but he wasn't going to be swayed.

Judge Reinhardt was a luminary judge, enjoying a reputation over many years on the bench as an advocate for liberal causes. The other judge had recently been appointed to the bench. She was young and not inclined to disagree with the venerable Judge Reinhardt. When I returned to my chambers, I told my law clerk that the judge was "as wrong as wrong could be" and we would write a dissent.

Months passed and I wondered when I would get Judge Reinhardt's anticipated decision. When I received it, I was surprised that it was simply a short, conclusory decision of a few paragraphs, devoid of analysis. I then wrote an extensive dissenting opinion explaining why I believed that Judge Reinhardt was wrong and attempted to alert the public to the dangers of trans fat in the hope that fewer unsuspecting consumers would jeopardize their health by buying Kroger Bread Crumbs.

I sent my dissenting opinion to Judge Reinhardt. As the presiding judge, he was responsible for having it filed, along with his decision. Once filed, the decisions would constitute the final disposition of the appeal. Kroger could continue selling its trans fat bread crumbs to an unsuspecting public.

But before he instructed his staff to have the decisions filed—which simply meant sending them to the clerk of the court—Judge Reinhardt said he wanted to take one last look at them. He would do that as soon as he returned from a scheduled doctor's appointment. He was running late and left in a hurry.

Sadly, Judge Reinhardt never made it back. He suffered a fatal heart attack at the doctor's office. The decisions were never filed. Judge Marsha Berzon was then randomly selected to replace him. After fully familiarizing herself with the briefs and listening to the recorded oral argument, she totally agreed with my memorandum and my dissenting opinion. The other judge then agreed, and my eighteen-page opinion reversing the district court then became the unanimous opinion of the court.[13]

The importance of the *Kroger* case cannot be overstated. It contributed to the national outcry against allowing trans fat to be contained in food products. But, if not for the circumstance of one judge having a fatal heart attack, unsuspecting consumers might never have known that they were ingesting a dangerous artificial food additive.

Such is how the law is made.

As for Donnell Drinks, the young adult I had read about in the *New York Times* article, he kept his case alive, without a lawyer, by "documenting his accomplishments in prison—articles he'd written, certificates he'd earned, thank-you notes from the nonprofits he'd raised money for—until he had three manilla envelopes' worth of records illustrating all the ways he'd grown," all of which came into play when he applied for early release.

The *New York Times* article told of another freed juvenile lifer. He said that he never felt "entitled" to be free and could not "wash the blood off my hands that's on my hands." But, the *Times* reported, "the emerging research, which showed brains aren't fully developed until people get into their 20s, gave him new understandings." It made him curious about himself: "I knew I was a good person, but I couldn't reconcile the person that I became and I know I am with the person that committed that horrible act."[14]

Even though Birkett, at eighteen, was not technically an under-age juvenile when he and Moore murdered Spence, I reduced his sentence from life to forty years. With 15% credit for good time, he would soon be released.

I held my breath the next day expecting to be taken to task by the press for letting a murderer out of jail. But much to my surprise, it never happened. Instead, a praiseworthy article appeared in the *Brooklyn Daily Eagle* by journalist Rob Abruzzese. I had never met or spoken to him and had no idea who he was. But a bold head-line read: "Lifetime in Prison to Freedom: Brooklyn Judge Frederic Block Grants Historic Release Under First Step Act." A large color picture of me appeared right below the headline and the article began by stating, "A beacon of hope shone through the Eastern District of New York's courtroom recently, as U.S. District Judge Frederic Block took a holistic approach to justice and granted Sher-win Birkett, a man who spent over half of his life in prison, a reduc-tion of sentence to just 40 years."

After explaining the First Step Act and recounting Birkett's crimes, the author wrote this about the judge:

> Judge Frederic Block, known for his meticulous and empathetic approach to justice, took up the challenging task of analyzing Birkett's request. A seasoned veteran of the bench, Judge Block has presided over multiple

high-profile cases and has been a staunch advocate for the compassionate application of the law. This commitment was evident in his approach to Birkett's case.[15]

10

JOE SMITH

Since I had let murderers sentenced to life out of jail under the First Step Act and was such a "compassionate" judge, should I not also have reduced Joe Smith's mandatory five-year sentence for receiving child pornography and let him go home to his wife and two young kids?

It didn't take long for him to file his motion. After just three months in jail, he asked that he be released because he was suffering from diabetes, which made him susceptible to contracting COVID-19. Since there were no cases of the virus at FCI Loretto, where he was housed, I denied his request. I wrote, however, that his application was being denied "without prejudice to renewal if circumstances changed."

Four months later, he tried again. His lawyer, Zachary Margulis-Ohnuma, wrote, "Unlike at the time of the Court's earlier decision, FCI Loretto is now in a potentially deadly health crisis due to COVID-19." He explained that at that facility "the number of positive cases among inmates has increased from none to 56, and the number of infected staff has increased from none to eight within two months." Moreover, "[e]ven before these increases the courts began releasing inmates from FCI Loretto who were deemed vulnerable, including former Trump campaign manager Paul Manafort, who was sentenced to seven years' imprisonment for financial and lobbying violations."

Smith's lawyer reported that his client's "health conditions have only worsened since his original motion" because of the rapid increase in his type 2 diabetes glucose levels and the failure of the jail to provide him "with a glucometer or another means of monitoring his sugar level."

Margulis-Ohnuma added that Smith had "used the time since his arrest in 2015 to rehabilitate his behavior" and wrapped up his single-spaced eight-page letter in dramatic style:

> [Smith] has gone through hell in almost eight months in prison, five of them in a pandemic. Continued confinement at Loretto presents such a high risk of death or serious injury that it cannot be justified by the need for further punishment or incapacitation. Under all the facts and circumstances, compassionate release should be granted.

Not surprisingly, AUSA David Gopstein took issue with most of what Smith's lawyer had written. First, Gopstein reported that the prison's medical records disclosed that "according to the defendant's most recent test, his average blood glucose level for the past three months (between May and August) was just below what it was when he started serving his sentence." And as to Smith's treatment, Gopstein wrote that "the defendant's medical records indicate that BOP [Bureau of Prisons] continues to treat and monitor defendant's diabetes, including by changing his prescriptions."

Gopstein did not "minimize the risk that COVID-19 presents

to inmates, and especially to inmates like the defendant who have medical conditions that place them at greater risk from COVID-19." He also acknowledged that "Type II diabetes may be, depending on an individual's age, health, ability to provide self-care and other individualized factors, an extraordinary and compelling circumstance that could justify a court's exercise of discretion to grant a requested reduction of sentence." But he argued that "[i]n the four months since the Court denied the defendant's first motion, there has not been a change in circumstances warranting a reduction of the defendant's five-year mandatory minimum sentence to the seven months he has currently served." Gopstein wrapped up his multipage submission by concluding,

> For the reasons set forth at sentencing and in the government's opposition to the defendant's first motion for compassionate release, a nearly 90% reduction in the defendant's 5-year mandatory minimum sentence to the approximately seven months he has served for the receipt of child pornography would not serve the purposes of sentencing under 18 U.S.C. §3553(a). Because there has not been a change in circumstances that would warrant the defendant's immediate release, the defendant's second motion for compassionate release should be denied.

Because of counsels' dueling contentions, I held a telephonic hearing. We were not conducting proceedings in court at that time because we were at the height of the pandemic. I had arranged to have an epidemiologist also on the phone. Dr. Melvin Kramer had reviewed the medical records and confirmed that Smith was suffering from serious diabetes and questioned whether his blood glucose level was being properly monitored.

After fully discussing Smith's second compassionate release

motion with counsel and having listened to Dr. Kramer's concerns about whether Smith's glucose level was being properly tested and monitored, I ruled, "I'm not going to be releasing him. I don't see him at imminent risk right now."

However, I was concerned about his welfare and subsequently ordered the Bureau of Prisons to "forthwith provide the defendant [Smith] a personal monitoring device and the necessary medical materials needed for the defendant to use the device three to five times per day to check his blood glucose levels." I further ordered that the bureau provide Smith "with diabetes education regarding the proper management of his blood sugar levels and diabetic condition." Finally, I added that the bureau shall have Smith "evaluated by a board-certified endocrinologist with a sub-specialty in diabetes in order to determine what further treatment in required."

At my suggestion, the order I issued was jointly drafted and proposed by the government and defendant's counsel. In the final analysis, Smith would be serving his full sentence, but his medical needs would not go unattended. During the height of the pandemic, I thought this was a sensible balance between enforcing the law requiring the imposition of the mandatory minimum and addressing the medical needs of a sick human being.

11

THE MAFIA CASES: ANTHONY RUSSO

So did I let Anthony Russo out of jail? And what would you have done?

In September 2022 I held a hearing to listen to the government and Russo's lawyer. The government was represented by Assistant U.S. Attorney Devon Lash. She had appeared before me in other cases, and I always found her to be very capable and forthright. But she was a zealous advocate for the prosecution.

Russo's lawyer was James Froccaro. He had also appeared before me on numerous occasions and was typically very well prepared and respectful. And he was an even more zealous advocate than AUSA Lash. Today would be no exception.

Russo was not there. The defendant was not required to appear in court for a compassionate release hearing—although he could if he wished. Froccaro told me his client was presently housed at a minimum-security federal facility in Allenwood, Pennsylvania. It would have been a big imposition and expense for the marshals to bring him to Brooklyn. I was glad that Russo did not require them to do that.

Russo would be turning seventy in six months and had been incarcerated for the past thirty years.

Right from the start, I wanted to find out from the government if Russo had been the triggerman on the two murders. I never got the answer from Lash. Although Russo was present when Minerva and Imbergamo were killed and was equally culpable for their murders, he may not have been the one who killed them. But he was also charged with numerous conspiracies to murder many members of the opposing family faction.

The Second Circuit Court of Appeals had just affirmed a decision by my colleague Judge Eric Komitee, who had denied a compassionate release motion by Mafia boss Victor Orena. I asked Froccaro, "How can I look beyond that in this case?"

Froccaro was ready. He rose from his chair and spoke in a clear, forceful voice. "It's pretty easy," he began. He had read the circuit court's decision and correctly told me that Orena was "personally responsible for basically all of the deaths because he was the reason for it." That, in Froccaro's opinion, "really distinguished Vic Orena from all the others."

Lash took issue with Froccaro's placing the primary blame for all the internecine murders on Orena. "It doesn't just take the boss, the man at the top to cause this death and destruction," she began. "It takes the person below that person to order other people, it takes the person who drives the car and pulls the trigger." She took a breath before finishing: "All of these people were responsible for the events that happened."

I spent the next several minutes listening to the two excellent lawyers go back and forth. Froccaro said that the average sentence for crimes entailing murder in the country was about twenty years, that Russo had rehabilitated himself while in jail, that he had been assessed by the Bureau of Prisons as a low risk for recidivism, and that he was subjected to harsh conditions of confinement because of the COVID-19 pandemic.

Lash was quick to respond. She asked me to put myself in the shoes of Judge Sifton back in 1992 "and imagine what the sentencing judge was looking at at that time." She rattled off bone-chilling statistics: "A dozen people died after this war, three of them were innocent bystanders. People that were caught in the crossfire." She reminded me that the city "was aflame," that "FBI agents had confiscated dozens and dozens of weapons and were simply trying to stem the violence in any way that they could."

Speaking of Russo, she emphasized that "[h]e was ordering people to look for opposing members of the crew and kill them if they were to find them, and he successfully did that with two men, ending their lives." She then did not hesitate to challenge me by arguing that because of the seriousness of Russo's crimes, which warranted the life sentence, "this Court needs a very good reason to be able to take that and commute it."

The lawyers then referenced other cases that they contended supported their respective positions. For example, Froccaro spoke about a case where the defendant was the leader of a heroin trafficking enterprise and "was responsible for at least five brutal and calculated murders aimed at eliminating competitors, informants, and witnesses." Nonetheless, he continued, the judge released him from his lifetime sentence, without parole, at the age of sixty-seven, "based upon pandemic-related concerns, and a showing that he had been, by all accounts, a model inmate, and an active and devoted father and grandfather."

Lash then pointed out that there are cases "that go the other way."

She was certainly correct. But I was curious and wanted to see "where we are today in terms of how these things have shaken out; those which were granted relief, those which weren't granted relief where murder has been involved." I then mused, "It's basically somewhat arbitrary whichever way you look at it, I guess?"

I told AUSA Lash, "I'm going to take a look at all [the cases], the ones that you cite, the ones that Mr. Froccaro cites." I continued, "I want to try to get an overview of where we're at here."

I thanked the lawyers for their efforts and returned to my chambers. I asked my law clerks to get me all the cases cited by the lawyers in their written submissions. I had to decide whether Russo had satisfied me that his circumstances were "extraordinary and compelling" and then whether the requisite balance of considerations that I had to perform under the First Step Act, including measuring the nature of his murderous crimes with his personal characteristics, warranted countermanding his lawfully imposed life sentence.

The central question I mulled during the two months that I took to decide the case was whether it would be presumptuous to override Judge Sifton's decision. He was, after all, one of the court's most liberal sentencers, but from reading the minutes of his sentencing hearing, he did not seem to have any qualms about putting Russo away for life.

Yet now, the First Step Act required me to decide if Russo was entitled to a second chance.

On November 2, 2022, I issued my decision in a twenty-nine-page written opinion. I started by commenting that "[t]his December will mark the fourth anniversary of the passage of the First Step Act." I then reported that "the Act has spawned a plethora of litigation which now makes up a significant part of a district judge's criminal docket." Indeed, I had a large backlog of compassionate release motions to decide. Obviously, I could not do them all at once, and there were other civil and criminal pending motions that were stacked up. But I certainly could not fault the prisoners for trying. They had nothing to lose. But this placed an extra burden on judges.

Nonetheless, I wrote that "[a]t the heart of the matter is the challenge the district judge faces in deciding which factors the judge can consider in determining whether the 'extraordinary and compelling reasons' threshold has been satisfied," and "[t]his has produced inconsistent caselaw across the country."

I embraced the Second Circuit Court of Appeal's decision in *Brooker*, which I was duty bound to follow. I noted that the guidelines required a defendant to be "at least 65 years old . . . experiencing serious deterioration in physical or mental health because of the aging process" and to have served "at least 10 years or 75 percent of his or her term of imprisonment, whichever is less."

Although Russo had been incarcerated for more than thirty years, he was not suffering from physical or mental deterioration; therefore, under this language, his incarceration could not satisfy the "extraordinary and compelling" threshold bar.

In *Brooker*, where the circuit court stated that the district judge has "broad" discretion "as in all sentencing matters" to fashion a proper resentence under the First Step Act, it provided some minimal guidance, such as recognizing that it would be appropriate to consider a defendant's extensive rehabilitation if it were coupled with "an unusually long sentence." But, as I wrote, "district courts throughout the country have not been provided with any guidance as to the limits of their 'broad' discretion . . . [and] *Brooker* did not address under what circumstances the district court would exceed its compassionate release discretion."[1]

I then had to row my sentencing boat into these uncharted waters and decide what to do with Anthony Russo.

Russo had principally argued that he was entitled to compassionate release because of his extraordinary rehabilitation. I agreed. He had not committed a single disciplinary infraction in the past twenty-one years, and, as I wrote, "[g]iven the realities of incarceration in a federal penitentiary, particularly under the specter of a life sentence, this record can only be viewed as exemplary." While he was incarcerated, Russo had also completed more than forty educational courses, obtained his GED, and "maintained a steady work assignment with a glowing review from his supervisor." In addition, the Bureau of Prisons rated his risk of recidivism as "minimal."

But the most convincing evidence of his rehabilitation and character were the two letters that Russo submitted from staff members at FCC Allenwood, each referring to him as a "model inmate." One was from Senior Officer Cody Leon, who wrote that "Mr. Russo has consistently shown a desire to not only better himself and the people around him but to improve his environment and community to the best of his abilities." He added that Russo was "considerate, respectful, trustworthy, and hard-working" and believed that he should be "given a second chance."

The other letter was from Recreation Specialist Ryan Shuck. He reiterated Officer Leon's sentiments, adding, "Mr. Russo has been one of the best workers and best men that have been employed by our department."

I found these letters "nothing short of commendable." But under the law, since I could not rely on rehabilitation as the sole factor to warrant compassionate relief, I had to determine if there were other factors that I could consider in combination with Russo's rehabilitation.

But what were these other factors?

The COVID-19 pandemic was relevant, and conditions in FCC Allenwood during the pandemic had made Russo's time incarcerated more punitive than anticipated at the time of sentencing. For example, nearly twenty-four-hour lockdowns had been imposed for long stretches to prevent the virus's spread; thus, Russo was not permitted to have visitors for over a year. While these measures were aimed at protecting inmates from illness, they also had, as I wrote, "an indisputably punitive effect."

All those who had sought compassionate relief from me under the First Step Act had spent some time at the Metropolitan Detention Center (MDC) in Brooklyn, or at the Metropolitan Correctional Center in Manhattan. These are the local federal facilities where prisoners who have not been given bail are housed pending trial. Those who have been convicted are also housed there for short-term sentences or until they are designated to a long-term facility.

Russo was housed at the Manhattan facility from 1993 until 1999, before he was transferred to his permanent facility at Allenwood. He had told his lawyer that the conditions at the correctional center during his confinement were inhumane. "Bed bugs and rats were everywhere" as well as "every species of roaches." He had "shared many a bed with rodents."

It was not his imagination. After the infamous Jeffrey Epstein was housed there for his "sexcapades," he committed suicide on August 21, 2019. The prison was soon thereafter closed because of its deplorable conditions and inadequate security. Over seven hundred of its prisoners were transferred to the Brooklyn facility.

Brooklyn's MDC is one of the largest federal lockups in the country, housing more than 1,600 people, but was hardly an improvement from the horrendous living conditions in Manhattan. To this day, when most of my colleagues and I render our sentences, we consider lowering the sentence for those who have been subjected to the deplorable conditions at New York's miserable jails.

A recent exposé of Brooklyn's detention center occurred during the Sam Bankman-Fried trial. Bankman-Fried was the founder of the bankrupt cryptocurrency exchange FTX and had initially been jailed at that facility by Manhattan Southern District judge Lewis

Kaplan for tampering with witnesses while free on a $250 million bond. His lawyer had pleaded with Judge Kaplan not to send him there. As reported by Reuters, "In recent years, MDC had been plagued by persistent staffing shortages, power outages and maggots in inmates' food" and "[p]ublic defenders have called conditions 'inhumane.'"

Reuters also reported that "[i]n the winter of 2019, an electrical fire cut off the jail's lighting and heat for days as temperatures fell to near zero Fahrenheit (minus 18 Celsius)." Moreover, "[l]awyers for [Ghislaine] Maxwell, who was convicted of recruiting and grooming teenage girls for abuse by Jeffrey Epstein, said raw sewage seeped into her MDC cell." Her attorneys compared the conditions there "to Hannibal Lecter's incarceration in the 1997 movie 'The Silence of the Lambs.'"[2]

The blackout crisis was not an isolated incident. As the *New York Times* reported in February 2019, it was just "the latest episode in a long history of neglect and brutality at the jail, one that has been documented in previous Justice Department reports." The *Times* further reported that "[i]nvestigators over the years have issued findings that suggest the jail is among the worst in the federal system, determining at different times that prisoners have been beaten, raped or held in inhumane conditions." The newspaper quoted from an interview with a former warden at the jail, Cameron Lindsay, who said that over the last decade "the M.D.C. was one of the most troubled, if not the most troubled facility in the Bureau of Prisons."[3]

And, as Maxwell reported, it is not just the male prisoners who are subjected to these inhumane conditions.[4] In October 2016, 161 women were held at the facility in two large windowless rooms with no fans. My colleague Magistrate Judge Cheryl Pollak has been reluctant to send female defendants there because of the "unconscionable" conditions. As reported in a 2016 *Daily News* article, Judge Pollak was troubled by a report from the National

Association of Women Judges, rendered after a 2015 visit by several female judges, which concluded that "[t]he absence of fresh, clean air, the complete absence of sunlight, and the absence of ANY outdoor time and activities are immediate issues which [the Bureau of Prisons] has failed to address in any meaningful fashion."

Judge Pollak was appalled. She commented in a court proceeding in October 2016, "I would like to get to the bottom of this before I remand anyone to MDC," adding that "[s]ome of these conditions wouldn't surprise me if we were dealing with a prison in Turkey or a Third World Country." Subsequently, she refused to send female defendants there who might otherwise have been candidates for incarceration.[5]

More recently, on January 3, 2024, Manhattan Southern District Judge Jesse Furman refused to send a convicted defendant to the MDC pending his sentence. He noted that the defendant, who had been free on bail, would have been subject to mandatory detention upon conviction because of the nature of his crime but cited a provision of the Criminal Code that allowed him to find "exceptional reasons" for allowing a convicted defendant to remain free until sentencing. He reasoned that the pervasive inhumane conditions at the MDC qualified as such a reason.[6]

In December 2023 I spoke with Michael Padden, a senior trial lawyer for the Brooklyn federal defenders office, who frequently visited the Brooklyn and Manhattan facilities to meet with his clients. He confirmed that the conditions at the Manhattan jail when Russo was there, as well as the current conditions at the Brooklyn jail, "are and were intolerable." As for Brooklyn, he told me that "there are frequent unexplained lockdowns that prevent family visitations, the plumbing is always faulty, toilets are always backing up flooding the cells," and that his defendants "are always at serious risk of physical harm because of frequent, uncontrolled gang fights."

The city's federal facilities are not the only blight on its inability to provide humane housing conditions for its prisoners. Rikers Island, which houses state defendants, is scheduled to be closed by August 31, 2027. As of August 1, 2023, 87% of its population—5,403 individuals—were detained there *pre-trial*, not even having been convicted of anything.[7] More than 50% were Black.[8] Rikers is being shuttered because it was plagued by understaffing, gang violence, crumbling infrastructure, an influx of contraband, and prisoner deaths—nineteen in 2022 alone.[9] The fatalities, and years of failed reforms, have led to increased calls for a federal receiver to take over the Department of Corrections.

Thus, in addition to Russo's extraordinary rehabilitation, I considered the harsh conditions of his six-year confinement at the Metropolitan Correction Center and the punitive nature of his confinement at Allenwood. I also considered that his advanced age, high cholesterol, high blood pressure, and borderline diabetes placed him "at increased risk if he were to contract the virus."

I wrote that "at the time Judge Sifton sentenced Russo, the sentencing guidelines were mandatory," but they now were discretionary. Therefore, "[t]his circumstance alone probably can be considered extraordinary and compelling to support the Court's 'broad discretion.'" I added that "in any event, it certainly can be considered a factor in combination with the other prevalent factors." I noted that, although *Brooker* was not retroactive, "as the government points out," it does not preclude "consideration of a significant post-sentencing change in the law as an extraordinary circumstance" since the sentencing court had no other choice at that time, before the guidelines were held in *Booker* no longer to be mandatory.

Next, I focused on the so-called trial tax. Just like Birkett, Russo had exercised his constitutional right to trial. Of his fourteen codefendants, seven also went to trial. Six were convicted and received mandatory life sentences under the then mandatory sentencing guidelines. The seventh was acquitted. While going to trial is a gamble since the government invariably has the defendant dead to rights, the fact that one of the defendants was acquitted shows that insisting on a trial, instead of pleading guilty, is hardly an idle gesture.

Of the seven codefendants who pled, their sentences ranged from approximately four years to 270 months (over twenty-two years). In general, the crimes committed by many of those defendants were no less violent or destructive than the crimes committed by those who received life sentences. For example, Theodore Persico, who pleaded guilty to multiple charges, including conspiracy to commit murder, received a 270-month sentence. And codefendant Richard Fusco, who was also charged with conspiracy to commit murder, was sentenced to 168 months.

I acknowledged that "[t]he argument can plausibly be made that no one convicted of murder should ever have their sentence reduced, and that when a judge sentences a defendant to life for murder the judge intends that the defendant should die in prison." I gave as an example Judge Komitee's decision in *Orena*, where he held that, even though the Colombo family crime boss had satisfied the extraordinary and compelling threshold given his poor health and advanced age, the judge "considered his murder convictions to outweigh the §3553(a) factors, and therefore denied his compassionate release application."

I wrote, however, that "[e]ven though I am similarly troubled by the fact that Russo orchestrated two murders," I did not "subscribe to that unyielding punitive concept in this case for a number of reasons." First, I asked the rhetorical question: "If the Government in offering its plea deals did not believe that all those indicted on murder charges should be sentenced to life, why should the court?"

Next, my research disclosed that the "sentences resulting from plea deals that the government entered into align with the national average for murder convictions." I found a decision that Chief Justice Roberts had written a few years ago where he noted that a life-without-parole sentence "was far more severe than the average sentence imposed on those convicted of murder or manslaughter, who typically receive under 25 years in prison." And the Sentencing Commission had also kept track of the murder sentences, noting that, for fiscal years 2015–21, the median sentence for murder was 240 months.

I reasoned, of course, that "[t]hese statistics support the notion that murders are not homogeneous" and "there are different types of murders with different degrees of culpability." I gave as examples "murders of passion and murders of revenge."

In Russo's case, the murders "were not directed at the public at large but were internecine executions of ruthless gang members." The mantra of the turf war between the rival Colombo factions many years ago was "kill or be killed." Therefore, Russo's release many years later, his advanced age, and the Bureau of Prison's assessment that he was a "minimal" risk of recidivism satisfied me that he was "unlikely to pose a danger to the public, satisfying the sentencing goal 'to protect the public from further crimes of the defendant.'"

I then commented again about Russo's extraordinary post-sentence rehabilitation, "even though he believed, prior to the advent of the First Step Act, that he would be spending his life behind bars." I thought that rewarding defendants for their rehabilitation while in jail was a "win-win." Knowing that it could possibly lead to their early release would encourage prisoners to behave and would make it easier to supervise them. Thus, I considered Russo's extraordinary rehabilitation as the most important reason to give him a second chance. If not for that, I might not have granted him any relief.

I did not believe that Russo should die in jail, and I reduced his lifetime sentence to thirty-five years.[10] With 15% good-time credit, he would be released in a few months, at the age of seventy. Not surprisingly, Russo was elated that after three decades he would be reunited with his family. His wife told his lawyer that "every Sunday at mass she lights a candle for Judge Block."

I believed I had written a thoughtful and well-reasoned opinion but suspected that I would be fodder for the yellow journalists who feed on reporting decisions by judges that they believe will sell papers to their tough-on-crime readers. I was right.

On the same day I vitiated Russo's lifetime sentence, I had let Paul Moore, Birkett's codefendant, out of jail. The two cases made a bold full-page headline in the *New York Daily News*: "2 Killers Get Break." Underneath was the subheading: "Judge: Law Allows Compassionate Release of Mobster and Drug Fiend," and a picture of a bullet-ridden car with the caption: "Two men were shot dead on orders from mobster Anthony Russo in March 1992." At the bottom of the page, the reader was told, in bold yellow type, to "SEE PAGE 5."

On that page, the newspaper factually recounted the major portions of my opinion but added that "[Judge Block] had a reputation for shooting from the hip and was ripped on the front page of the *New York Daily News* in 2007 with the headline 'Judge Blockhead' after he ridiculed prosecutors for seeking the death penalty against a drug kingpin during a racketeering murder trial."[11]

This so-called reputation was the handiwork of the *New York Daily News* reporter who covered the courts. John Marzulli was a Judge Block junkie. Whenever there was a slow news day, he would write something about things I had said in court. Although I never thought I shot "from the hip," I was perhaps somewhat more outspoken than my fellow judges about things that happened in court that troubled me.

The death penalty case against Kenneth "Supreme" McGriff, the "drug kingpin" gratuitously referenced in the *Daily News* article, was one example. McGriff had been indicted with several others for being part of a criminal organization whose members and associates engaged in murder, narcotics trafficking, and money laundering. McGriff was the kingpin of this gang of criminals, and the government sought to put him to death because of his involvement in the murders of two drug rivals, one of whom had killed McGriff's best friend and the other who was rumored to be arranging to kill McGriff before Supreme could get revenge.

Rather than dirty his hands by doing the actual killings, McGriff hired four others to murder them for the princely collective sum of $25,000. However, the government did not seek the death penalty against them; instead, it allowed those killers to enter into cooperation agreements, and three of them testified against Supreme at his trial.

Whether the federal government should seek the death penalty was a hot-button topic at that time. Since McGriff was the leader of the gang, the U.S. attorney general decided he should be put to death. The local U.S. attorney's Brooklyn office was tasked with the responsibility to handle the prosecution. This would, in effect, require two trials before the same jury, each requiring a unanimous verdict. First, it would have to decide if the defendant was guilty. If so, there would then be a second, lengthy trial to decide if the death penalty should be invoked.

During the guilty phase of McGriff's trial, it became clear to me that there was no realistic chance that a unanimous jury would vote to put him to death. The victims were drug dealers; one had killed McGriff's best friend, and the other was plotting to kill McGriff before he could seek revenge. Moreover, McGriff did not personally kill them, and those who did—although at his behest—testified against him in exchange for cooperation deals to save their own necks. They were an unscrupulous lot, led by a wanton killer nicknamed "Manny Dog," who made his living killing people for money. They were arguably better candidates for the death penalty.

Since it was apparent to me and, I suspect, to the government as well that the prosecutors would simply be wasting everybody's time and valuable judicial resources, as well as the taxpayers' money, I suggested to the prosecutors that they ask the attorney general whether he still wished to seek the death penalty. The jurors were not present at the time. I told them to "kindly advise Washington that in this judge's opinion, there is not a chance in the world there would be a death penalty verdict in this case." I added that the government's effort to seek McGriff's execution was "absurd" and that it would be a "total misappropriation" of taxpayer funds, saying, "If I'm wrong, I will have egg on my face, but I will not be incorrect."

The attorney general refused to reconsider his decision. Because of the complex and protracted nature of a death penalty phase, the prosecutors, in my opinion, wasted the next several days presenting its useless case. The jurors then had to decide whether to put McGriff to death.

It took the jurors less than an hour—over lunch—to do what everyone following the case believed would happen. They rejected the death penalty in favor of life imprisonment. On the verdict sheet the jurors had to report how many found that there were specific mitigating factors that contributed to their decision. The results reinforced my belief that it was a complete waste of time and judicial resources to seek the death penalty against McGriff. For example, five jurors believed that the favorable plea agreements offered to the cooperating witnesses weighed against the imposition of the death sentence; seven thought that the murders were motivated, in part, by McGriff's sincere belief that the victims were out to kill him; eleven considered that the victims contributed to their own deaths by voluntarily choosing to engage in violent criminal conduct; five believed that McGriff had proved himself capable of acts of generosity and kindness; four thought that he was otherwise attempting to move his life in a positive direction; and nine were of the opinion that his life had value.

To this day, the *New York Daily News* refers to me as Judge Blockhead. Although my colleagues always deny that their decisions are ever influenced by the press since "they have lifetime tenure," none of them would ever want to see their names on the front page of any newspaper in a derogatory manner.

Judges are vilified and attacked all the time, and they must take it as part of their calling. There are many unfortunate recent examples of attempts to hold federal judges and the judiciary in disrepute. But we march on trying objectively to apply the rule of law. And we are ever so grateful that the Founding Fathers (I suspect the Founding Mothers were whispering in their ears) had the foresight to create an independent judiciary by providing for lifetime appointments to ward off attempts to politicize the third branch of government.

I do owe the *Daily News* a debt of gratitude, however. It motivated me to write an op-ed for the *New York Times* explaining to the public the need for responsible and intelligent decisions by the attorney general about which cases should be selected for the death penalty. I explained that, given the enormous costs and demands to the judicial system, it was being unduly burdened with death penalty prosecutions.

The *Times* ran the piece, together with a line drawing of a condemned man and the headline "A Slow Death." The article drew the attention of the *New York Law Journal*, which reported that the recent surge of death penalty cases in New York had rankled lawyers because of the "lack of death sentences, and the high cost of those trials." It also reported that Senator Feingold had cited the article during a Senate Judiciary Committee hearing when questioning a district court nominee on her views about the death penalty. Moreover, Supreme Court Justice John Paul Stevens cited it with approval in one of his opinions.

I had pointed out in my op-ed piece that the taxpayers had to foot the bill for both the costs of prosecution as well as the costs of defense. Moreover, in death penalty cases, two lawyers are usually assigned pro bono, at taxpayers' expense, to represent the defendant. Like almost all death penalty defendants, McGriff could not afford a lawyer. I pointed out that the vouchers submitted by McGriff's defense team exceeded $500,000, and assuming the costs of prosecution to be at least equal to that, $1 million would appear to be a fair estimate of the costs of the death penalty phase of his trial. If there had been a death verdict, the costs of appeal would have added millions.

I concluded, therefore, that taxpayers had spent about $17 million for the seventeen federal death penalty trials in New York State through 2007, with only one death verdict to show for it—which was reversed on appeal. Thus, they would be footing the $9 million bill for the prosecution of McGriff and the eight other death penalty cases that were scheduled to be tried in my courthouse.

I explained that all this came at a time when the federal judicial system was struggling with unprecedented budgetary cuts, but that costs were not the only concern. It takes about three weeks just to select a death penalty qualified jury and months to try the case— as it did in McGriff's case. This would mean that the eight judges of my court at that time—approximately one-third of today's bench—would be hard-pressed to do the rest of their judicial work. The prosecutor's office would have the same problem. The enormous amount of time consumed by death penalty prosecutions would deplete the office's resources and its ability to attend to its backlog of non–death penalty cases.

In writing my article, I was influenced by the thinking of the chief judge of the Ninth Circuit Court of Appeals, who was highly regarded by the conservative Federalist Society. He had given a speech where he noted that "the number of executions compared to the number of people who have been sentenced to death is miniscule." He concluded that "whatever purposes the death penalty is said to serve—deterrence, retribution, assuaging the pain suffered by the victims' families—those purposes are not served by the system as it now operates."

I agreed with the chief judge's conclusion that instead of overwhelming the courts with death penalty trials, the attorney general, in the discharge of his awesome responsibility, should seek the death penalty only for the most depraved killers, "lest the judicial system be overwhelmed, the community's will ignored and taxpayer dollars improvidently spent."[12]

I believe that the current attorney general has hued to that standard. He has sought the death penalty for only the most depraved crimes, such as the person who gunned down eleven worshippers at a Jewish synagogue in Pittsburgh.

I was pleased that my comments about the foolish death penalty prosecution of McGriff went public. Although I believe that most of my colleagues would have shied away from speaking about it and the economic realities of a death penalty prosecution, I am of a different mindset. Because judges acquire important information about the judicial system, I subscribe to the view that they have a moral responsibility to share their special knowledge with the public, and I am willing to run the risk of being called Judge Blockhead to do that.

In retrospect, I can appreciate the temptation of the headline writer for the *Daily News* in not passing up the opportunity to capitalize on my name. After all, "Judge Scaliahead" could never have worked, nor "Judge Ginsburghead," nor, perhaps, anyone else but me. What headline writer worth her or his salt could realistically pass up the opportunity to tack "head" onto "Block"? I still laugh about it. It's really funny. I feel bad about only one thing. My innocent grandchildren, Janice, Liam, and Bevin, may have to go through school being called "Little Blockheads."

Having let Anthony Russo out of jail, I then asked myself whether I should also do the same for Vittorio Amuso.

12

THE MAFIA CASES:
VITTORIO "LITTLE VIC" AMUSO

I can't blame Amuso for trying. He must have thought that since I let his fellow mafioso big shot out of jail, I might be "one of those liberal soft judges" and would let him spend his final days at home rather than in a prison hospital. And he was represented by a team of lawyers led by the same lawyer who had represented Russo.

James Froccaro wrote that his client was eighty-eight years old and that he was dying. His argument was riveting and made an enormous impression on me as I read his submission:

> While there is no debate that the underlying conduct was serious, there remains a fundamental truth that no person should be denied a death with dignity, even prisoners whom the Government cast as unworthy. In this regard, the government's opposition provides no convincing reason as to why an elderly and ailing prisoner, after serving an extremely long term of imprisonment, must medically suffer and ultimately perish in a prison cell when the Court possesses the perfect power, pro-

vided by the First Step Act, to compel the end-of-life
care of such a prisoner to his family.

The government's memorandum of law in opposition to Amuso's motion first recounted why he was serving a lifetime sentence.
It succinctly reminded me that he "was found guilty by a jury on
54 counts, including racketeering and racketeering conspiracy,
nine counts of conspiracy to commit murder or attempted murder
in-aid-of-racketeering, six counts of substantive murder-in-aid-of
racketeering, 34 counts of bribing labor officials, one count of conspiracy to bribe labor officials, one count of conspiracy to commit
extortion, and one count of conspiracy to evade income tax."

The government correctly explained that under the compassionate release statute, a district court may deny a compassionate release
motion "based solely on the §3553(a) factors, without reaching the
question of whether extraordinary and compassionate reasons are
present." It contended that such was this case because "[t]he nature
of Amuso's pervasive and heinous crimes, his ongoing affiliation
with the Lucchese Crime Family, and recent rulings in this district
denying compassionate release motions by similarly situated mob
leaders like Amuso all indicate that he must serve his life sentence,
as imposed."

First, the government emphasized that, as the leader of the Lucchese crime family, Amuso "commanded the hits to further his own
interests, protect the power he held as Boss of the organization,
and protect the interests of the organization itself." It emotionally
concluded that "[t]he effects of Amuso's actions are long-standing,
as the families of those slain at his command will never be able to
obtain the relief that Amuso now seeks."

The government also tugged at my emotions in a footnote commenting about Amuso's assertion that he "relies at times on a
wheelchair to navigate his facility." Calling this "ironic," the footnote recounted that "Amuso left 40-year-old victim Peter Chiodo

partially paralyzed and confined to a wheelchair after Amuso's hitmen attempted to murder him to prevent him from cooperating with the government against Amuso." It argued that keeping Amuso behind bars for life "serves the important need to deter other leaders of organized crime groups from resorting to violent and deadly means to reach their ends."

The government then contended that Amuso was still dangerous "because he is *still* the Boss of the Lucchese Crime Family." It wrote that "testimony by former Lucchese Crime Family soldier John Pennisi revealed that, as recently as 2017, Amuso orchestrated a leadership change in the Lucchese Crime Family from prison through the exchange of coded letters." Pennisi further testified that "following Amuso's order, the Brooklyn faction was prepared to kill various members of the Bronx faction in the event they did not comply with the order."

"In short," the government wrote, "Amuso's danger stems from his past and current position as the Boss of the Lucchese Crime Family, a violent organization that still exists today, and his ability to have others commit violent crimes on his behalf, as he did so many times before his arrest."

Finally, the government argued that Amuso's motion should be denied "because similarly situated mob leaders who engaged in equally or less egregious and heinous criminal conduct than Amuso's have also had their requests for compassionate release denied." It gave a few examples, including Judge Eric Komitee's decision denying the compassionate release motion of Victor Orena, the acting boss of the Colombo crime family, because Judge Komitee did not believe his serious medical conditions outweighed "the §3553(a) factors that supported his continued imprisonment."

The government also contended that, in any event, the "extraordinary and compelling" bar had not been met because it did not believe that Amuso's medical condition warranted that finding.

It wrote that "Amuso primarily argues that his arthritis, among other ailments, has diminished his quality of life and 'rendered him immobile.'" However, it continued, "[w]hile the Government does not diminish difficulties faced by elderly inmates, the conditions that Amuso details do not rise to the level of 'extraordinary and compelling circumstances' that warrant release." It added that "Amuso's conditions, while requiring individualized care, are not terminal and are not of the type that other courts have decided are sufficient to justify early release."

The government referenced a note from Warden Kelly of FCI Butner Medium II, who had denied Amuso's administrative compassionate release motion submitted through the Bureau of Prisons, relating that Amuso does not have a terminal illness, is independent with his self-care, does not have a debilitated medical condition, and has his current medical conditions under control. Moreover, the government pointed out that "Amuso does not allege that FCI Butner II is not providing him proper treatment for his conditions or that the facility is unable to accommodate his needs."

Finally, the government rejected the argument that the advent of COVID-19 cases at the facility had relevance: "Amuso has received both the COVID-19 vaccine and booster, thereby diminishing his likelihood of severe infection, and he does not articulate any unique risks of severe illness that he faces due to COVID-19."

In their response, Amuso's lawyers took issue with all the government's contentions. It first debunked the warden's "self-serving assessment" as lacking any "actual insight into the current severity of Mr. Amuso's medical condition, the attendant grim prognosis, and the daily and insurmountable obstacles that Mr. Amuso must overcome to provide self-care as an elderly sick, and immobile inmate within a secure federal prison."

Amuso's lawyers noted that the government's opposition "makes no mention of the fact that the facility housing Mr. Amuso was again on a long lockdown during the pendency of this motion (May 26th to June 19th) and that Mr. Amuso was confined to a prison cell during that entire time (notwithstanding his advance age, serious medical circumstances, and immobility)." They argued that the government's opposition "misses the mark in claiming that a compelling reason for compassionate release could not be collectively based on Mr. Amuso's advanced age (88), medical ailments, immobility, and his service of more than 30-plus years of imprisonment without incident."

Remembering what I had written in my *Russo* decision, I agreed that these collective circumstances sufficed to satisfy the "extraordinary and compelling" bar. I then read what Amuso's lawyers wrote about the government's conclusion that Amuso failed to satisfy the §3553(a) factors.

First, they referenced a recent decision from the Fourth Circuit Court of Appeals that resonated. As they correctly wrote, in that case "the Court explained that the district court could not fulfill its duty to reconsider the [compassionate release] factors by merely recounting the considerations that supported the original sentence." The court of appeals' decision explained that the compassionate release statute "necessarily envisions that the [compassionate release] factors may balance differently upon a motion for compassionate release than they did at the initial sentencing." The court pointed out that if a district court's original compassionate release analysis could always prove that a sentence reduction would intolerably undermine those factors, the statute would have no meaningful effect.

This logic made sense to me. Amuso argued, therefore, that "[w]hile the government attempts to exclusively focus on factors considered by the sentencing judge more than 31 years ago, it errantly ignores Mr. Amuso's *current* circumstances, perfect institutional record, and the powerful comments provided by the many people who have remained in contact with him during his imprisonment—all of which weigh heavily in favor of compassionate release."

Amuso's lawyers then argued that "the government ignores all of the legal precedent cited in Mr. Amuso's moving papers, namely a multitude of cases in which compassionate relief was granted to much younger prisoners notwithstanding equally serious offense conduct." Then they took issue with the government's claim that sentencing disparities were meritless. Amuso had cited in his moving papers that several "similarly situated mob leaders" who engaged in "equally" heinous conduct had been released, and none were older than seventy-two.

Finally, Amuso's responsive submission attacked the government's reliance on the testimony of cooperating witness John Pennisi to support its conclusion that Amuso was still issuing murder orders from jail. They pointed out that Pennisi admitted that he had never spoken to Amuso and, for many reasons, that his testimony was totally unreliable and self-serving.

In summation, Amuso's lawyers wrote: "For the many reasons set forth in Mr. Amuso's moving papers and herein, the Court should grant the instant application for compassionate release, because Mr. Amuso's advanced age, severe chronic medical conditions and immobility, along with his service of 31-plus years of imprisonment, provide a compelling reason for such a humane outcome."

Amuso's motion papers were so complete and his lawyers' memo so well written and thought provoking that I did not believe I needed to have them regurgitated to me in court. I had enough information to decide whether I should let Vittorio Amuso die at home.

* * *

The press was all over the case. I probably shouldn't have read any of the papers before I put pen to paper, but my law clerks had placed some of them on my desk, and I guess curiosity got the best of me. I believed, however, that I was sufficiently inured over the years to the press that I wouldn't be influenced about what they wrote about Amuso's compassionate release motion.

Typical was the *New York Post* article with the headline "Former Mafia Boss Vittorio Amuso, 88, Convicted of Ordering Several Murders Pleads for 'Compassionate Release' from Prison." The paper published a picture of Amuso in handcuffs after his arrest in 1991 and quoted extensively from his lawyers' filings, including their principal contention that "Mr. Amuso's life expectancy is grim, and his advanced age and deteriorating health render his remaining quality of life negligible." The *Post* noted that "[t]he filing comes as the latest from a string of aging Mafiosos pleading for compassionate release under the First Step Act of 2018."

The article generated lots of comments. Some of them were clever and made me laugh, but all but two of seventy-one said Amuso should remain in jail. Someone named Trigger Happy wrote: "The man is 88 years old, violent thugs get out earlier than that more often. And this is the Mob we're talking about, I'm sure the people *someone else* killed weren't angels." Another had a nasty social and political bite: "What happened to 'criminal justice reform'? Or is that just for 'focus groups' and 'racial identity groups'?"

But the sixty-nine others were adamant that Amuso should remain behind bars. Typical were the following: "I'm not inclined toward mercy for a crime boss who ordered and arranged multiple murders. 'Life in prison' does mean all of it." Many were less literate: "He should be wheeled to the edge of a bottomless pit and pushed in"; "Shoulda juiced him"; "He'll be dead by the time you get his victims to agree to let the scum out"; "Give him family visitation, then kick his ass back into his cell."[1]

But one thing was clear to me. I would be brutalized by the media if I let Vittorio Amuso out of jail. It would make "Judge Blockhead" look like child's play.

I didn't do it. I would like to think that the vicious negative media reaction, which surely would have happened, had nothing to do with my decision, but I wonder to this day whether my subconscious was at work, and I did not want to see "Judge Blockhead" in print once more. To be sure, I had rendered other unpopular decisions during my three-decade judicial career, as judges must do. Being a devout practitioner of the rule of law, I would like to believe that I would do the same again in Amuso's case if I thought it was the right decision. But one never knows!

The two key considerations for me were Amuso's health and his potential ongoing involvement with the Lucchese crime family, given the range of the serious crimes for which he had been convicted. In both cases, I felt the facts weighed against granting Amuso compassionate release.

In determining whether Amuso's health condition qualified as "extraordinary and compelling," I considered the detailed list of his claimed medical conditions, which included nuclear sclerosis, hypertension, hyperlipidemia, coronary atherosclerosis, cardiac arrhythmia, anemia, an eyelid disorder, a conjunctival disorder, teeth loss, hematuria, benign hypertrophy of the prostate, enthesopathy, hearing loss, osteoarthritis of the knees, and severe osteoarthritis of the hips. I was also aware that his arthritis of the hips caused him severe pain and that he required a wheelchair to move around his facility and assistance from other inmates or staff to pick up his food trays and make his bed. I also recognized that Amuso's condition and affect had declined in recent months and that he was recently designated a "Care 3" inmate because of his increased need for regular medical care.

In my opinion, I acknowledged that "Amuso, like many elderly inmates, faces particular difficulties while incarcerated" but concluded, nonetheless, that his medical records "reflect that the [Bureau of Prisons] is managing Amuso's medical conditions adequately by providing him with medications, x-rays, and medical appointments upon his request." I then noted that "[a]lthough his affect has decreased in recent months and his hip and knee pain have increased, he has not received a terminal diagnosis, nor has he endured any prolonged hospital stays."

Amuso had also cited "the risk of COVID-19 to his health as an elderly inmate." But I wrote that although he had twice contracted the virus, he had recovered both times and was now vaccinated. I cited cases supporting the proposition that "[c]ourts typically deny compassionate release to vaccinated defendants." And as for his lockdown during the pandemic, I noted that "with the pandemic's abatement, this circumstance is also lessened."

Finally, I concluded that other reasons listed by Amuso—his age, the time he had served, and his rehabilitation—"do not tip the balance toward finding that extraordinary and compelling circumstances exist." I reasoned that Amuso's advanced age and his thirty-one years in prison "are the product of his life sentence, rather than extraordinary and compelling circumstances."

I then addressed the possibility of Amuso's ongoing criminality and that Pennisi had stated that "Amuso had orchestrated a leadership change in the [Lucchese] organization from prison in 2017." I acknowledged that Amuso vigorously denied this assertion and that the Bureau of Prisons deemed him to be a minimal recidivist risk. I also considered his argument that he had "a flawless incident report, and that with the support of his family, as evidenced by their numerous letters of support, he poses no risk of slipping back into a life of crime."

I reasoned, however, that "[a]lthough it is certainly commendable that Amuso has remained incident free over the course of his incarceration," even if the court assumed that Amuso had not participated in any aspect of the Lucchese family during his incarceration, the extent of his criminality argued against release. I cited with approval Judge Komitee's decision in *Orena*, stating that "[f]ollowing the adoption of the First Step Act, a strain of cases . . . has emerged in which the offenders' criminal history is so long, and their victims so numerous, that even serious health conditions do not suffice to merit relief." I believed that Amuso's case fell "squarely in that category." Regardless of whether Amuso met the extraordinary and compelling circumstance bar, I concluded that he utterly failed to satisfy the §3553(a) factors.

I therefore concluded that, "[g]iven the depth and breadth of Amuso's role in the Lucchese Family, and the harm exacted on both individuals and the community, the Court cannot in good conscience reduce his sentence. His conduct was simply too serious, too disrespectful of the law, and too destructive to the fabric of society to warrant anything other than a life sentence."[2]

This time the *New York Daily News* did not refer to me as Judge Blockhead. It simply quoted from my conclusion but added some spice to the article by writing about the shoving of the dead canary down Bruno Facciolo's mouth "to warn anyone else of the consequences of singing to the feds."[3]

In an extensive article in *The Messenger*, one of Amuso's lawyers, Anthony DiPietro, was reported as telling the blog: "Justice should never be built on getting even, and there remains no legitimate reason in America for an extremely elderly and sick inmate to remain imprisoned when they can no longer walk and provide self-care." He was sharply critical of my decision, adding that "[t]he sea change from such an inhumane and costly reality, which the First Step Act was meant to cure, failed today."[4]

I wondered whether he was right.

Shortly after, my lawyer friend Paul Bergman sent me an opinion piece by Katie Engelhart, a contributing writer for the *New York Times Magazine*, who had written extensively on dementia and aging. The heading immediately captured my attention: "I've Reported on Dementia for Years, and One Image of a Prisoner Keeps Haunting Me." She had visited the Devens Federal Medical Center in Massachusetts, where Victor Orena was housed, and had met him. Engelhart reported that Orena thought he was the warden and would tell the prison staff, "I'm the Boss. I'm going to fire you." She later observed that on one occasion "Mr. Orena sat in his wheelchair beside a man with bloodshot eyes." She asked them "if they knew where they were." Orena replied, "I don't remember, I don't know."

Since my decision denying Amuso's compassionate release motion had relied on Judge Komitee's *Orena* decision, I was eager to read the rest of the article. At the outset, Engelhart wrote of speaking with Timothy Doherty, a senior specialist at the detention center, who helped run the prison's Memory Disorder Unit. It was the federal prison system's "first purpose-built facility for incarcerated people with Alzheimer's disease and other forms of dementia." Doherty told her that 90% of the men he oversees "don't know what they did" and "[s]ome of them don't even know where they are." Engelhart then wrote about the prisoner she met who still haunts her. As a result of cognitive impairment, he no longer remembered his crimes but was "still being punished for them."

This animated Engelhart to delve into the wisdom of warehousing aging prisoners, like Orena, suffering from dementia. She trotted out some statistics, first noting that "[w]e don't know exactly how many people in American prisons have dementia because nobody is counting," but reported that "[b]y some estimates, there are already thousands, most of them languishing in the general population."

She wrote, "Older adults represent one of the fastest-growing demographic groups within American correctional facilities. Between 1999 and 2016, the number of prisoners over 55 increased by 280 percent, according to a report by the Pew Charitable Trusts; over the same period, the number of incarcerated younger people grew by just 3 percent." She attributed this to "tough on crime" reforms in the 1980s and 1990s, "which lengthened sentences and ensured that many more people would grow old and frail and then die behind prison walls."

Engelhart then examined the rationales for keeping the demented in jail. As for the need to protect the public from dangerous criminals, she noted that the men in the Mental Disorder Unit "are very sick and confused and use wheelchairs or walkers, and they probably couldn't hurt anyone if they wanted to"; moreover, "researchers have found that recidivism rates drop to nearly zero for people over 65."

As for the possibility of in-prison rehabilitation, Engelhart rationally noted that "with dementia, there is no rehabilitation." As she logically explained: "Moral education is impossible for a person who cannot be educated. And a prisoner cannot reflect on his crimes—and then maybe regret them or feel ashamed of them or be repulsed by them or resolve to do better in the future—if he does not even remember them or feel responsible for them."

Engelhart interviewed Patricia Ruze, the clinical director of the prison. She did not believe that the men in the Mental Dementia Unit "posed a threat to anyone." She thought "it would be 'totally appropriate' to release the whole unit on compassionate grounds and relocate the men to community nursing homes, which already have experience dealing with aggressive behaviors brought on by cognitive impairment—and which cost much less than operating a prison unit."

I agreed with Ruze's conclusion: "In this country, we incarcerate way too many people for way too long. We give people life sentences.

And then they turn 90, they're in diapers, they get demented. We have to ask ourselves, what are we accomplishing?"[5]

I have asked myself that same question many times, especially after I recently read *Correction: Parole, Prison and the Possibility of Change*, a provocative book written by the investigative journalist Ben Austen. In it he reports that the arrest rate for people over fifty is "less than 2 percent," and for people sixty-five or older, "it is nearly zero." Thus, "[t]he truth is that the United States could let out nearly everyone in prison over fifty-five and see very little statistical change."

Austen posits the question: "How could anyone claim that the point of incarceration was to incapacitate the truly dangerous when there are more people older than fifty-five in U.S. prisons (165,000) than there are people in high-crime range of eighteen to twenty-four?" He notes that "[m]any of these older prisoners were convicted of violent crimes when they were young," as Sherwin Birkett was, "and they are now serving extremely long sentences or life without parole."[6]

Of course, there are those who believe that such punishment is entirely appropriate and that such people should never be given a second chance. But I am not one of them.

After I finished reading Engelhart's profound article, as well as a good part of Austen's book, I wondered again whether I should have let Amuso out. Engelhart made a lot of good points and sensitized me to the complexities of managing an aging prison population and the lack of justifications for keeping demented old criminals in prison. Austen reports, for example, that "[g]eriatric health care in prison is both disgraceful and expensive" and "[i]t costs, on average, three times more to incarcerate an older person than a younger one."[7] I reasoned, however, that Amuso, unlike Orena, was not demented and still belonged behind bars.

13

THE MAFIA CASES: ANTHONY "GASPIPE" CASSO

On November 10, 2020, Anthony Casso submitted a twenty-page memorandum skillfully prepared by his lawyer James D. Arden, a partner at the prestigious and expensive Sidley Austin law firm. Arden had to spend a lot of time writing it, and I wondered how Casso was able to retain the services and pay for such a high-end law firm.

In the memo, Arden wrote that "Mr. Casso is a 78-year-old, wheelchair-bound man serving a life sentence at USP Tucson. He has prostate cancer, coronary artery disease—for which he had been awaiting a heart operation—kidney disease, hypertension, bladder disease, and respiratory issues associated with a history of smoking." Casso had also recently tested positive for COVID-19 and was "currently hospitalized due to severe respiratory problems."

From a health point of view, Casso was in worse shape than Amuso, and if anyone should be released for medical reasons, he was a perfect candidate.

Thus, Casso's lawyer argued that, although Casso was not

sentenced to death, "he remains at serious risk of death due to COVID-19 if he remains incarcerated." The attorney emphasized Casso's long list of serious medical conditions and correctly stated that "[n]umerous courts have recognized that significant health problems in the face of the COVID-19 pandemic constitute 'extraordinary and compelling' reasons" for compassionate release.

Moreover, as Arden noted, Casso was jailed "at a COVID-19 hotspot" because "153 inmates at USP Tucson [were] currently positive for COVID-19—the fourth highest number among federal prisons." Given Casso's fragile physical condition, Casso's lawyer logically wrote that his client's release to home confinement would not pose a danger to the community.

Primarily, Casso's lawyer drilled down on Casso's many comorbid physical ailments. He stated that "[i]t is well known that individuals suffering from cancer are at a heightened risk of experiencing severe complications, including death from COVID-19." And he referenced statistics about Casso's other ailments: that individuals with hypertension experience a 58% increased risk of inhospital mortality from COVID-19 and those with chronic kidney disease had a "50% higher chance of suffering in-hospital mortality from COVID-19." Arden concluded his analysis of Casso's medical woes by arguing that because Casso "suffers from *all* of these conditions" he "faces a heightened chance of experiencing a severe outcome from his COVID-19 infection."

Casso's dire health clearly passed the "extraordinary and compelling" bar, but I was curious about how his lawyer would present the required additional factors—which are known, once again, as the §3553(a) factors—that would support his release. Casso's lawyer tried his best. He cited everything from Casso's "characteristics" and "the nature and circumstance of the offense" to "provide just punishment for the offense," the need for the sentence to "promote respect for the law," to "afford adequate deterrence to criminal conduct," to "protect the public from further crimes of the defendant," and to "provide the defendant with needed educational or vocational training, and medical care." He correctly added that courts also consider "whether a defendant is a danger to the community." Finally, he reasoned that "[k]eeping Mr. Casso in prison would not serve these objectives; he no longer has ties to his former life of crime, and his advanced age and lack of mobility make it unlikely that he will be involved in any future criminal conduct."

In conclusion, Arden wrote: "Mr. Casso's continued incarceration puts him at grave risk of not surviving his current fight with COVID-19. The extraordinary and compelling circumstances of Mr. Casso's situation, coupled with the *totality* of the requisite additional factors, outweigh the factors related to his past criminal history and conduct."

Not surprisingly, the government took issue with Casso's contentions. AUSA Keith Edelman's response was well written, and in twenty-four pages left nothing to peradventure.

The crux of it was twofold. First, Edelman disagreed that Casso's failing health, including the risk of dying from COVID-19, should warrant an "extraordinary and compelling" finding. As he argued: "All defendants sentenced to life in prison will, at some point, begin to succumb to one disease or another, or suffer from failing health due to old age." He continued: "[T]hat Casso is presently suffering from severe symptoms relating to COVID-19—a disease that has killed millions around the globe and over 250,000 in the U.S. alone—does not transform his case into one that is 'extraordinary and compelling.'"

The government also maintained that Casso's "motion to release must be denied because he remains a danger to the community." It posited that "his conviction of over 25 murders, his attempts to escape from custody, [and] his plots to murder both the presiding judge and prosecutor" hardly support his claim that he is no longer a danger. Edelman reasoned, "Casso did not himself personally commit many of the crimes of conviction. For instance, as underboss, Casso's role was to advise and support the boss (Amuso) in the management of the organization and the myriad crimes it committed." In other words, "Casso's danger stems from his position within the Lucchese crime family, a violent organization that still exists and carries out crimes to further its objectives, and his willingness to end another's life without hesitation." Thus, "although Casso is wheelchair-bound, elderly and suffering from COVID-19, this does not mean that he cannot have others commit violent crimes on his behalf, as he did time and time again before his arrest."

While I recognized the government's concern, I thought that Edelman really nailed it when he addressed the additional factors.

First, he wrote that, as for the "nature and circumstances of the offense[s]," they "could not be more serious."

> Casso, as second-in-command of one of the most violent criminal organizations in the country, committed various crimes on its behalf—including over 25 murders, multiple other attempted murders and murder conspiracies, extortion, bribery, corruption and other offenses. Indeed, the murders of conviction (and the others, if they had also been charged) are so serious that Congress has decided that regardless of his criminal history or background, a defendant convicted of even one such offense (let alone over 25) must serve the rest of his life in prison or be executed.

Edelman argued that Casso had simply attempted summarily to whitewash his violent criminal past, which included "plots to kill a federal judge and prosecutor that thankfully never came to fruition." In sum, he argued that the "nature and circumstances" of the offenses "weigh severely against any form of compassionate release and, in the government's estimation, alone preclude granting the instant motion." He put a dramatic coda to his argument by writing that "the decades of criminal activity Casso committed" and his wanton disrespect for the law "would severely undercut respect for the law and would not provide just punishment."

Thus, the government concluded that Casso's failure to meet the §3553(a) factors "outweigh[ed] the purported 'extraordinary and compelling reasons' warranting release, and so, Casso's motion must be denied."

I agreed. I issued a simple, one paragraph electronic text order:

> The Court has carefully considered the gravity of defendant Anthony Casso's medical condition. But even assuming it presents an extraordinary and compelling circumstance, the Court finds, in light of the nature and extent of defendant's criminal history, that he remains a danger to the community and that the §3553(a) factors do not justify early termination of his life sentence. Therefore, Anthony Casso's motion for compassionate release is denied.

Casso and his lawyer weren't kidding about his health. On December 16, 2020, a lead metro headline of the *New York Post* announced, "Ex-Lucchese Underboss Anthony 'Gaspipe' Casso Dies After Getting COVID-19 in Prison." It reported that "[t]he 78-year-old-mafioso—who sought and was denied compassionate release last month—died Tuesday." It explained that just three weeks before, I had denied his compassionate release motion.

I didn't feel any guilt. As the *Post* recounted, Casso was known as a "homicidal maniac," was "one of the most violent bosses of the city's five crime families," and was "believed to have slain at least 36 people."[1]

And I wondered if Casso had remembered that he threatened to kill me or if his lawyer knew that. Because of Casso's deteriorated health, he probably forgot. But it really did not matter. Even if he had not wanted to murder me, I would have rendered the same decision. He was simply the "worst of the worst" and was not more deserving than the short shrift I made of his compassionate release motion.

As I was putting the finishing touches to this part of the book, I came across a report from the Sentencing Project extolling the importance and virtues of the First Step Act. It struck me as the best way to end my shout-out for the act.

The Sentencing Project, a nonprofit "bridge" organization, partners with 68 national groups and over 150 state-level organizations in advocating for justice reforms. The statistics it had compiled from Department of Justice reports about the First Step Act were compelling.

Initially, the Justice Department reported that "between 2019 and early 2023, approximately 30,000 people have been released from federal prison before their original release date as a result of the First Step Act's reforms." The majority (58%) were serving time for a drug trafficking offense. Within this group, 13% had been rearrested or reincarcerated since their release. Comparatively, 57% of people released from state custody for a drug trafficking conviction recidivated within three years.

In addition to the inmates who were released by district judges exercising their compassionate release discretion, the others were the beneficiaries of the act's reduction of mandatory minimums, its crack cocaine reforms, its increase of good-time and earned-time credits, and its expansion of home confinement.

The act had also provided needed rehabilitative and educational opportunities. In that regard, the number of inmates who received GED or equivalent educational certificates doubled during the last year, and the wait list for literacy program instruction was presently over 28,500 people.

The Sentencing Project report explained why these reforms were necessary and concluded,

> The First Step Act was designed to be a multi-pronged solution to some of the most vexing problems of the federal prison system. The law expands opportunities for individuals to pursue rehabilitation and education, authorizes a range of early release mechanisms for eligible individuals to return to their families and communities, and makes retroactive the provisions of the Fair Sentencing Act of 2010 to reduce the disproportionate impact of especially harsh drug laws.[2]

* * *

I think it is safe to say that, at the federal level, the First Step Act has been a resounding success. But if we are effectively to address our mass incarceration problem as well as the other failings addressed in the First Step Act, it is imperative that the states also "step up to the plate."

PART IV
THE STATES

14

THE NEXT STEP

I hope the First Step Act will flourish and that all the federal courts—like the Second Circuit—will give it a "broad" reach. I also hope that, as its name suggests, there will be a Second Step Act and that Congress will enact more sensible sentencing reforms.

But since the states, rather than the federal government, house about 90% of our prison population, it is imperative that all the states take up the congressional cudgels and enact comparable First Step acts as well. Otherwise, our mass incarceration problem and the sentencing inequities addressed by Congress in its initial first step will persist.

A riveting example of the need for giving all our nation's judges—be they state or federal—the discretion to reconsider a sentence is a recent decision rendered by the Ninth Circuit Court of Appeals in *May v. Shinn*, upholding a morally indefensible lifetime sentence without parole imposed by the Arizona state courts.

I was still sitting as a visiting designated circuit judge for the Ninth Circuit, and in addition to my majority opinion in *Fitch* I had

authored seventeen unanimous opinions for the court—including
the *Kroger* bread crumb trans fat case—before the *May* case.

Sitting on the Ninth Circuit panel with me in *May* were Circuit
Judges Sandra Ikuta and Michelle Friedland. Both are extraordi-
narily capable judges and are committed to the rule of law.

On July 12, 2007, a jury in Maricopa County, Arizona, convicted Stephen May of sexual molestation of three children between
the ages of six and eight. He was acquitted of sexually molesting
another child, who was nine years old.

May was a swimming coach at a public pool, and the incidents
consisted of his allegedly briefly touching the children in their gen-
ital areas on the outside of their bathing suits or clothing. At the
age of thirty-seven, May was sentenced by the state trial judge to
seventy-five years of incarceration without parole. Unless he lives to
be 112, he will die in jail.

After several years of unsuccessfully bringing a host of post-
conviction proceedings and appeals in the Arizona state courts,
including being rejected by Arizona's high court, May brought a
habeas corpus proceeding in an Arizona federal district court. The
district judge granted his petition and released him. May had spent
the last ten years of his life behind bars before the judge set him
free. The judge reasoned that he had been denied a fair trial because
of his trial counsel's ineffectiveness. The state of Arizona was not
happy with the decision and appealed to the Ninth Circuit Court
of Appeals. I was troubled by the government lawyers' arguments
during the oral argument and asked a lot of questions.

What happened after that was bizarre. Initially, Judge Friedland
and I wrote a joint opinion upholding the district court's decision to
release May, although on different ineffective-assistance grounds.
The case was hardly a slam dunk. As we wrote, "The State's case
turned entirely on the jury's believing the testimony of several

child victims who all had struggled to provide details of the alleged molestation on the stand, including failing to remember whether some of the incidents even took place."

Not surprisingly, after five days of listening to all the conflicting evidence, and after deliberating for two days, the jury told the judge that it could not reach a verdict. The judge therefore declared a mistrial, dismissed the jury, and set the case down for a retrial several months later. But while the lawyers were putting on their coats and leaving the courtroom, the bailiff, who had told the jurors that they were discharged and could go home, came running back into the courtroom and told the judge that the foreperson asked whether they could try again to reach a verdict.

The judge told the lawyers that since a mistrial had been declared, they need not allow the jurors to resume their deliberations. Nonetheless, both the state's lawyer and defense counsel agreed to the resumption of deliberations. Apparently, May's lawyer thought that because of the weakness of the case there was a good chance of an acquittal and that it was worth rolling the dice rather than face the prospect of a retrial.

The dice turned out to be snake eyes.

Judge Ikuta, who has a reputation as a strict constructionist, dissented from Judge Friedland's and my opinion upholding the district court's decision to release May. She reasoned that the strictures of a recent U.S. Supreme Court decision severely limiting this kind of judicial review required us to defer to the decision of Arizona's highest court, which had affirmed the guilty verdict. The state then asked Judge Friedland and me—in a written motion—to reconsider our majority opinion.

Much to my surprise, Judge Friedland changed her mind and wrote an extensive opinion explaining why she was resigned to agreeing with Judge Ikuta. A short concurring opinion was written by Judge Ikuta explaining that her concurrence was based on "the limited scope of federal habeas review." But, surprisingly, Judge Friedland wrote a rather extraordinary separate concurring opinion "to express [her] dismay at the outcome of this case." It's short and poignant, and worth repeating in full:

> While I certainly recognize the seriousness of child molestation, the evidence that May was actually guilty of the five counts of molestation he was convicted on was very thin. May's conviction on those counts was based almost entirely on the testimony of children who were the alleged victims. Yet, as described in [my] opinion, that testimony had many holes. The potential that May was wrongly convicted is especially concerning because he was sentenced to seventy-five years in prison—a term that all but ensures he will be incarcerated for the rest of his life. . . .
>
> Given the significant constraints on the scope of our review, we are not in a position to do more than decide the narrow question whether the proceedings in this case were so egregiously unfair that they violated the Constitution. But I agree with the dissent that this case, and in particular May's sentence, reflects poorly on our legal system.

* * *

The thrust of my dissent was that May's counsel was guilty of ineffective assistance of counsel by not objecting to resumed jury deliberations because he blindly consented to allow the jury to continue with its deliberations after it had been discharged without "a meaningful consultation" with his client. I also explained that his decision was "anything but an informed decision." I wrote, therefore, that these failures, as well as reconstituting a discharged jury, violated the Supreme Court's law governing ineffective assistance of counsel claims.

I concluded my dissenting opinion by decrying that "the majority returns a man to prison—probably for the rest of his life—under the severe strictures of Arizona's sentencing regime."[1]

The Supreme Court, which annually accepts only a handful of cases for review, summarily denied May's certiorari application. He thereafter made another failed written attempt—before my panel—to vacate the new majority's opinion. This gave me an opportunity to write another extensive opinion. I wrote that the question of May's lifetime sentence rested on "the emotional overlay that contributes to irrational sentencing when the nature of the crime entails sexual misconduct involving children."

I ended with a pitch for May's sentence to be commuted. As I wrote: "I believe it is the responsibility of judges who have had the opportunity to identify injustices in the sentencing of a defendant to play an active role in sharing that information with those who will be passing final judgment on the life of a human being."

Clemency grants in Arizona are rare. They require a recommendation from the clemency board to the governor, but I realistically recognized that, "[g]iven the nature of his offense, it is unlikely that the Clemency Board would recommend that the Governor commute May's sentence."[2]

May, who had been at liberty for four years since the district judge let him out of jail, was a law-abiding citizen during that time. He never attempted to abscond even though he knew that if the district judge's decision were reversed he would be going back to jail.

Having exhausted all his legal options, May then voluntarily returned to prison for the rest of his life.

* * *

The *May* case points up once again the power of a single judge. If Judge Friedland had not changed her mind, May might very well be a free man today.

To be sure, I am hardly a big fan of those who molest children. They should be punished, and even severely. But it is, understandably, an emotionally charged crime and can result, as in this case, in an irrational sentence.

If Arizona had a First Step act, a judge would have the discretion to consider whether May should be spending the rest of his life in jail. You may disagree, but if I were that judge, I would reduce his sentence. The factors I have employed in handling my compassionate release motions—including May's exemplary prison record and the probable disproportionate sentence compared with other sentences for more egregious conduct—seem to resonate, especially because of the thin evidentiary record and the initial hung jury.

But Arizona does not have a First Step act. Moreover, in 1994 it abolished discretionary parole for all offenses committed on or after January 1, 1994.[3] Instead, as part of its so-called truth-in-sentencing law, its legislature mandated that individuals serve at least 85% of their court-imposed sentence. Thus, they would be eligible for earned-release credits that could shorten their sentences by up to 15%. In 2019, Arizona allowed those serving time only for drug offenses to serve 70% of the total sentence.[4] But before the truth-in-sentencing law, people in Arizona were parole eligible after serving *one-half to two-thirds* of the imposed sentence.[5] As the Prison Policy Initiative writes, the state's decision to abolish discretionary parole and replace it with mandatory parole "eliminates a powerful tool for hope and transformation."[6]

In any case, this law does not help May since, as Judge Friedland correctly noted in her concurring opinion, "a person sentenced for a dangerous crime against children in the first degree . . . is not eligible for suspension of sentence, probation, pardon or release from confinement on any basis . . . until the sentence imposed by the court has been served or commuted."[7]

It is easy to understand why the Prison Policy Initiative gave Arizona an F– grade in its evaluation of state parole systems. And it is also easy to comprehend why thirty-five other states received either an F– (fifteen) or an F (twenty). Notably, like Arizona, the sixteen states with an F– also had eliminated discretionary parole.

In grading each state's parole release system, the Prison Policy Initiative's report looked at factors including whether most people sentenced in the state were offered discretionary parole and whether people seeking parole were able to meet face-to-face with those evaluating their petition.

> Unlike what happens in the movies, most parole hearings don't consist of a few stern parole board members interviewing one sweating, nervous incarcerated person. Most states don't have face-to-face hearings at all, and instead do things like send a staff person to interview the prospective parolee. The staff person then sends a report to the voting members, who each vote (perhaps in isolation). The incarcerated individuals never have a chance to present their case or present their parole plans to the voting members or perhaps to speak to their crime or to rebut any wrong information the board may have. On the other hand, most states, by legislative mandate, give prosecutors and crime survivors a voice in the process.

Other considerations include the degree to which staff are permitted to assist with petitions for parole. As the report states further: "[M]any states have rules that prohibit correctional staff—who are often the only people who have had day-to-day contact with the incarcerated person and can speak to their behavior and to their recent on-the-job performance—from testifying at parole hearings."

Finally, the report evaluated parole systems based on their transparency. As the report explains,

> One of the strongest critiques of state parole systems is that they operate in secret, making decisions that are inconsistent and bewildering. Neither the individuals being considered for parole nor the general public understand how parole boards decide who to release or who to incarcerate further. When parole systems reject people for arbitrary or capricious reasons, they unintentionally, but to devastating effect, tell incarcerated people that their transformation does not matter. And the public, who is paying for the criminal justice system, deserves to know how it works and how well it works.

The report calls for uniform guidelines for considering parole and annual public reports that "explain deviations from outcomes recommended by parole guidelines." It also argues that "[i]ndividuals who are denied parole and fit all the requirements should be able to appeal based on objective factors."[8]

I agree with those sensible recommendations. But I would add that the states should follow Congress's lead and pass their own First Step acts. As the report makes perfectly clear, the parole system in the United States is broken, and in those sixteen states, such as Arizona, which no longer have any discretionary parole system and which limit good-time credit releases to those who have not committed the most serious crimes, prisoners such as Stephen May have absolutely no legal recourse.

Even in states that still grant parole, the grant rate is miniscule. For example, the *Alabama Reflector* reported in September 2023 on a finding by the Alabama ACLU that out of 267 parole hearings for eligible people from July to August, the Alabama Bureau of Pardons and Paroles had granted parole to only 7%, "a fraction of the grants from five years ago." Moreover, this rate was marked by significant racial disparities: about 4.7% of African Americans were granted parole, compared with 11.8% of comparable whites.[9] Such a low success percentage reminded me of the parsimonious grants of the Federal Bureau of Prisons, which is what initially led to the First Step Act's granting prisoners the right to bring their own compassionate release motions to a federal district judge.

The abject failure of the country's parole systems must change, and Congress has shown the path. It is time for all the states to emulate the federal First Step Act.

May also represents a case where an innocent man may have been convicted. Judge Friedland poignantly pointed out how shaky and questionable the evidence was; moreover, the jury was hung before the bizarre events leading to its renewed deliberations.

That a jury may get it wrong is particularly true in cases involving the most odious of accusations and is borne out by the thousands of documented exonerations. The most riveting example is that, since 1973, 195 innocent people on death row have been exonerated.[10]

But the innocent people on death row are only the tip of the iceberg. In a special report issued in December 2023, the National Institute of Justice—the research development and evaluation agency of the U.S. Department of Justice—estimated that nearly 5% of all convictions were of innocent people.[11] Some studies go as high as 6%.[12] These numbers are likely conservative because the studies can measure only the wrongful convictions we know about. But if even 1% of the people in prison today are innocent, 19,000 are languishing in a cell when they should be free. If it were 5%, it would be an astonishing 95,000 innocent people.

The most prominent organization dedicated to freeing innocent people, the Innocence Project, was founded in 1992 by Barry Scheck and Peter Neufeld, who gained national attention in the mid-1990s as part of the "Dream Team" of lawyers who formed the defense in the O.J. Simpson murder case. While the project's initial mission was to free wrongfully convicted defendants using DNA evidence, it has expanded into the country's major nonprofit institution committed to overturning wrongful convictions.[13]

The National Registry of Exonerations, founded in 2012, compiles data on exonerations in the United States beginning in 1989. As of December 2023, the registry lists 3,442 convicted defendants who were exonerated through DNA and non-DNA evidence, reflecting over 31,070 years of imprisonment.[14] I had one such case.

Jabbar Collins spent sixteen years in jail after being wrongfully convicted of murdering a Hasidic rabbi. The Hasidic community had demanded that the Brooklyn DA quickly find the killer or risk losing the critical political support of that community of over two hundred thousand voters—who always voted in a bloc. The DA charged his chief prosecutor, Michael Vecchione, with the task, and Vecchione quickly obliged. At the trial in 1994, three witnesses lied and said that they made no deals with the prosecution in return for testifying against Collins. Vecchione was the trial prosecutor. He not only failed to correct the record but ridiculed the claim in his closing argument to the jury that such deals had been made.

In 2010, my colleague Judge Dora Irizarry required the prosecution to produce withheld documents that described how Vecchione had threatened and manipulated the witnesses and eventually struck deals with them for their false testimony. She then set Collins free. Collins then brought a civil lawsuit against Vecchione and New York City for monetary damages. That case was assigned to me.

I was compelled under the law to conclude that Vecchione was entitled to absolute immunity from suit.[15] However, the case against the city could go forward because under the law it was responsible for Vecchione's unlawful conduct. Rather than face the horrible press that a public trial would surely have engendered, the city settled the case for $10 million. Collins thereafter collected another $3 million from the state.

Collins put his money to good use. He founded and became the president of Horizon Research Services, a consulting firm that provides legal research and writing services to attorneys. He also became an active member of It Could Happen to You (ITCHY), a New York–based criminal justice reform nonprofit dedicated to serving the needs of the falsely accused and wrongfully convicted. At its annual 2018 dinner, Collins presented me with ITCHY's Ken Thompson Minister of Justice Award.

On May 30, 2023, New York City mayor Eric Adams appointed Collins as one of three members to the city's Commission to Combat Police Corruption. In announcing the appointments, the mayor commented, "These appointees are committed to ensuring all members of the NYPD, and the institution itself, are held to the highest ethical standards, and we thank them for answering the call to service."[16]

The *Collins* case spawned a new era for New York State in coming to grips with its wrongful conviction problem. In 2015, the long-term incumbent Brooklyn DA had been defeated for reelection to a seventh term by the charismatic Ken Thompson, who campaigned for the end of wrongful convictions. Soon after Thompson was elected, he established a three-member independent committee to flush out other wrongful convictions. Sadly, he passed away—at the age of fifty—just two years after he became New York City's first African American district attorney.

But Thompson left a legacy. To date, over five hundred Brooklyn wrongful convictions have been overturned.[17] Many of the falsely accused, like Collins, were young Black men who had been in jail for over ten years before they were freed. Ron Kuby, a well-recognized civil liberties lawyer, handled many of these cases and told me two years ago that the city had paid these people a total of about $400 million for their suffering. It has undoubtedly paid much more since then.

Other New York counties followed Brooklyn's lead and have overturned the convictions of many wrongfully convicted defendants. Moreover, through the joint lobbying effort of the Innocence Project and ITCHY, the state legislature has established the country's first—and only—State Commission on Prosecutorial Conduct. As part of that effort, I was asked by the Innocence Project to write an op-ed piece for the *Daily News* supporting the commission's creation. I agreed.

In 2018 I had written a commentary for the Marshall Project, a nonprofit news organization that covers the criminal justice system, titled "Let's Put an End to Prosecutorial Immunity." I had recounted the Jabbar Collins case and explained why I gave Vecchione prosecutorial immunity. I explained that I was bound to follow a 1981 Second Circuit Court of Appeals' precedent, written by then circuit judge Irving Kaufman (who had imposed the death penalty against Ethel and Julius Rosenberg when he was a federal district judge). Judge Kaufman's decision concluded,

> The falsification of evidence and the coercion of witnesses . . . have been held to be prosecutorial activities

for which absolute immunity applied. Similarly, because a prosecutor is acting as an advocate in a judicial proceeding, the solicitation and subornation of perjured testimony, the withholding of evidence, or the introduction of illegally seized evidence at trial does not create liability in damages.

Judge Kaufman's rationale was that "these protected activities, while deplorable, involve decisions of judgment affecting the course of a prosecution."

I questioned the soundness of this dated law. As I wrote,

[The] solicitation and subornation of perjured testimony, the withholding of evidence, or the introduction of perjured testimony, the withholding of evidence, or the introduction of illegally-seized evidence at trial are not "decisions of judgment"; they are truly "deplorable" intentional acts—the antithesis of the exercise of judgment. Professional prosecutors, charged with the awesome responsibility of faithfully applying the law to guard against innocent people being convicted of crimes they did not commit, should be held accountable for such conduct.

Therefore, as I concluded, "the cloak of absolute immunity should judicially or legislatively be lifted." But sadly, regardless of a groundswell of support by many reform-minded organizations, it has yet to happen.[18]

My article in support of the creation of the State Commission on Prosecutorial Conduct was published in July 2018 by the *Daily News*, the same newspaper that had called me Judge Blockhead. I wrote that the legislation had passed both the state senate and the assembly with bipartisan support, and if passed into law, the commission would "have the power to investigate citizens' allegations of prosecutor malfeasance and recommend sanctions." I wrote about the *Collins* case: "As a federal judge for over two decades, the level of prosecutorial abuse and lack of accountability in this case has haunted me," and while the taxpayers have paid $13 million to Collins, "[t]he prosecutor hasn't paid a dime, nor has he been punished at all for his egregious behavior."

I therefore recommended that Governor Cuomo sign the legislation into law, which he did.[19] After an unsuccessful effort by the state's District Attorneys Association to block its implementation, the commission was established in 2021. It consists of eleven nonsalaried members appointed by the governor, the majority and minority leaders of the legislature, and New York State's chief judge. It is still in its developmental stage, with a small recommended budget for fiscal year 2024 of $1.75 million, but at least it is a step in the right direction.[20]

That innocent people have spent years in jail because they were wrongfully convicted is a black stain on our criminal legal system. A 2020 special report of the National Registry on Exonerations detailed bone-chilling stats:

- Official misconduct contributed to the false convictions of 54% of defendants who were later exonerated. In general, the rate of misconduct was higher in more severe crimes.
- Concealing exculpatory evidence—the most common type of misconduct—occurred in 44% of exonerations.
- Black exonerees were slightly more likely than whites to have been victims of misconduct (57% to 52%), but this gap was much larger among exonerations for murder

(78% to 64%)—especially those with death sentences (87% to 68%)—and for drug crimes (47% to 22%).

- Police officers committed misconduct in 35% of cases. They were responsible for most of the witness tampering, misconduct in interrogation, and fabricating evidence—and a great deal of concealing exculpatory evidence and perjury at trial.
- Prosecutors committed misconduct in 30% of the cases. Prosecutors were responsible for most of the concealing of exculpatory evidence and misconduct at trial, and a substantial amount of witness tampering.
- In state court cases, prosecutors and police committed misconduct at about the same rates, but in federal exonerations, prosecutors committed misconduct more than twice as often as police.[21]

Other statistics particularly resonated with me as the dissenting judge in the *May* case. The 2022 Registry's annual report notes that one-third of all exonerations involved crimes that never happened. This was particularly prevalent in child sexual abuse cases—like *May*. Of the 312 exonerations for that crime, 78% were "no crime cases," meaning that no assault had ever happened.[22]

Finally, an additional report from the National Registry of Exonerations confirms that wrongful convictions are a pervasive national issue—not simply confined to Brooklyn and the other New York counties. It reported that from 1989 to March 2021, state and municipal governments throughout the country have "paid more than $2.9 billion in compensation—$756 million in statutory awards for wrongful imprisonment and almost $2.2 billion in judgments and settlements in civil lawsuits." But unfortunately, "55% have received nothing."[23]

* * *

If we are to pride ourselves on being a just and fair society, we obviously need the best mechanisms to guard against sending innocent people to jail. I believe from my experience on the bench that jurors truly try to get it right. I am constantly impressed with how seriously they take their awesome responsibility to adjudicate the guilt or innocence of a fellow human being charged with a crime. But, like all of us, they are not infallible.

The First Step Act offers a much-needed corrective. At least federal judges can now review sentences and determine if a prisoner is deserving of a second chance or should never have been convicted in the first place. As the *May* case shows, the states must now allow its judges to do the same.

On January 9, 2024, I received a letter out of the blue from Stephen May's parents, Patricia and Terry Borden, thanking me "for recognizing the injustice" in their son's case. The opening paragraph stated, "It gave us and our son . . . hope that an Arizona Clemency hearing would prevent him from dying in prison."

But the next paragraph was disheartening: "Despite your compelling memorandum highlighting all the injustices in Stephen's case, the Clemency Board denied a recommendation to the Governor for Clemency."

I was disappointed but not surprised. As I had written in my second decision recommending that May be granted clemency, "[g]iven the nature of his offense, it is unlikely that the Clemency Board would recommend that the Governor commute May's sentence."[24]

Accompanying the two-page single-spaced letter were three other letters that had been submitted to the clemency board. Two greatly troubled me. The first was from juror #1, who believed during the initial jury deliberations "that Stephen May [was] innocent, as there was no evidence to prove his charges." The juror wrote that, "After the shock of being brought back into the room and the exhaustion of deliberating for such a long time, I felt pressured to change my vote." He was critical of the foreman, who had stated that "he is a father" and May "was guilty just by being there." Nonetheless, juror #1 had caved after the foreman "delivered a riveting speech upon returning to the room along the lines of 'we can do this, and he probably will only get a year or two, let's compromise and just do guilty on a couple of the counts.'"

This was not the only post-verdict juror note expressing second thoughts about the efficacy of a guilty verdict that I have seen during my long tenure on the bench, and I am loathe to revisit a jury verdict barring extraordinary circumstances, such as proof of jury tampering. I recognize the importance of closure and respect the juries' verdicts. But the May case was so unusual—and, once again, as Judge Friedland ruminated, an innocent man may have been wrongly convicted—that I was struck by the guilt that this juror had carried with him seventeen years after he rendered his compromise verdict. As he told the Clemency Board:

> To this day, it makes me sick to my stomach thinking about that case. I understand the role of a parent is to protect their children, but I believe that those children were injured by their parents and the legal system and not Stephen May.
>
> I ask this Board to recommend that the Governor commute Stephen May's sentence to correct this injustice. I do not believe he deserves to spend the rest of his life in jail. I live with guilt that he had to spend any time in jail at all based on my weakness to adhere to the rules of the court despite the peer pressure of the foreman and parents in the jury box.

Another letter was from the widow of Dr. Arnold P. Gold, a prominent founder of the specialty of pediatric neurology. As Ms.

Gold reports, her husband had treated Stephen since he was a baby "due to ataxia and involuntary movements of his head and extremities (hands and legs), and a worrisome large head." This caused Stephen "to be hospitalized four times before he was four years old, at the Babies Hospital in New York City" where Stephen "was an active patient until 1988, at age 17." Stephen was described at age eight by a medical expert as "clumsy, bumping into things, falling and unsteadiness," and "had difficulty as a schoolchild due to his appearance and the intermittent shaking of his head, legs and hands."

Ms. Gold explained that at Stephen's trial, "No expert was called upon to provide testimony and information to the jury regarding Stephen's brain anomalies and involuntary movements" because his lawyer mistakenly thought that Dr. Gold was dead. Ms. Gold was "ready to travel to Arizona to share with [the Clemency Board] personally and under oath" what she was writing in her letter.

My curiosity got the best of me, and I wanted to learn the reasons why the Clemency Board turned May down. I thought his parents would know, and in any event I wanted to ask their permission to publish the letters. When I reached them on the phone, I told them that I was writing a book about giving prisoners a second chance and had decided to dedicate it to their son. They told me that as God-fearing Christians they "always had faith that our justice system would do the right thing."

Stephen's parents had a transcript of the hearing before the Clemency Board. I asked them to send it to me. The chair stated at the beginning that "the legal standard is a very high standard," and that "the board will only recommend a reduction in sentence if, after finding by clear and convincing evidence, that the sentence imposed is clearly excessive." A board member then summarized the case, describing the five incidents that were the bases of May's convictions, namely, briefly touching the children on their private parts on the outside of their clothing.

The board member stated that, "The purpose of Mr. May's request for Commutation is based on his assertion that there was no sexual intent," that "[h]e suffers from a neurological disorder that causes clumsiness, if you will, and he claims innocence." Moreover, "he feels a collective 75 years of incarceration for touching children outside their clothing is excessive, if not extreme." The board member acknowledged that in May's "detailed application, there is much commentary on regretful jurors, disagreeing judges, and outraged supporters, but little discussion in the way of aberrant behavior or traumatized children." He found it "troubling that Mr. May does not express concern for the victims, even if his pattern of touching children inappropriately was accidental." Nonetheless, he wanted to hear what the other board members had to say before he made his decision.

The chair then spoke again. Her comments were short, noting the "irregular and unusual" nature of the case and the mistrial, and that "there's a lot of things that happen that I think are concerning." However, she concluded that, "given the nature of the offenses," it was just "not possible" for her "to find that the sentence is excessive."

The third board member just said, "I agree." But the last member spoke in support of clemency. She concluded that there was "no evidence of sexual motivation," that she did not "see Mr. May as a sex offender." She apparently had read Ms. Gold's letter because she stated that May "had issues that caused shaking in his hands." She commented that, "I don't know that I've ever seen a case considering all the letters that have been written"; and that "he was released for four years or so, [a]nd then had to come back." She further commented on all the good things he accomplished for the community while he was at liberty for those four years, and that "he certainly didn't resist coming back to incarceration." She was in favor, therefore, of "moving to a phase two commutation hearing where other people can come in and speak."

But this would never happen because the other three members simply voted to deny recommending clemency.

As I finished reading these minutes I thought once again about why the Prison Policy Initiative gave Arizona's parole system an F-grade. But I was particularly troubled that May's clemency application was doomed to fail because he did not comment on the abuse he allegedly inflicted on the children; he believed—as did juror #1 and the one dissenting board member—that he was innocent. We now know that thousands of innocent people are wrongly convicted, and it is simply counterintuitive that they should nonetheless confess to, and express remorse for, a crime they did not commit as the price to pay for getting out of jail.

I hope that the three members of the Clemency Board who voted against giving Stephen May a public second-phase hearing will not take umbrage at what I have written but accept that we are all in the justice business and should always keep an open mind to revisit a previously rendered decision that may not have been providently made. I have done that, and I hope the Arizona Clemency Board will be like-minded.

POSTSCRIPT: COLLATERAL CONSEQUENCES

Regrettably, the First Step Act does not address the egregious failure of the federal judicial system to eliminate a little more than a thousand irrational collateral consequences it attaches to formerly incarcerated individuals after they have served their sentences and regained their freedom. But more appalling are the *multi*-thousands of nonsensical and counterproductive collateral consequences the states impose on their formerly incarcerated people. Removing such impediments to rejoining society is the best way to attack our country's enormous recidivism rate.

Until I read Michelle Alexander's book *The New Jim Crow* a few years ago, I had no idea of the breadth and reach of the collateral consequences facing formerly incarcerated individuals. But I then came across a running inventory by the American Bar Association of our nation's collateral consequences. I was astonished to learn that there were then nearly 50,000 federal and state statutes and regulations that impose penalties, disabilities, or disadvantages on those convicted of felonies once these people have served their time and have been released from jail. Of those, nearly 1,200 are the product of federal law (300 for controlled substance offenses); the remaining 48,800 come from the states, which, once again, are responsible for roughly 90% of the prison population.

As Professor Alexander explains, "Myriad laws, rules, and regulations operate to discriminate against ex-offenders and effectively prevent their reintegration into the mainstream society and economy. These restrictions amount to a form of 'civil death' and send the unequivocal message that 'they' are no longer part of 'us.'" As she wrote,

> Today a criminal freed from prison has scarcely more rights, and arguably less respect, than a freed slave or a black person living "free" in Mississippi at the height of Jim Crow. . . . A criminal record today authorizes precisely the forms of discrimination we supposedly left behind—discrimination in employment, housing, education, public benefits, and jury service. Those labeled criminals can even be denied the right to vote.[1]

Alexander's polemic motivated me to take a hard look at these collateral consequences, which resulted in a lengthy opinion I wrote in 2016, *United States v. Nesbeth*, explaining why I sentenced a young woman to probation instead of to jail. It triggered my thoughts about "civil death" under the English common law. I had read a decision by the New York Court of Appeals written in 1888, in which a convicted felon in old England was "placed in a state of attainder." It explained that of the several consequences of being in such a state, the attained person "is disabled to bring any action, for he is *extra legem positus* and is accounted in law *civilter mortus*." Thus, "he is disqualified from being a witness, can bring no action, nor perform any legal function; he is in short regarded as dead in law."

In the United States, civil death has never been imposed by common law; it has always been a creature of statute.

Chevelle Nesbeth had been convicted after a jury trial of bringing six hundred grams of cocaine into the country. While visiting Jamaica at the behest of her boyfriend, she was given two suitcases by friends, who had purchased her return airline ticket, and was asked to bring them to an individual upon her arrival to the United States. As disclosed during the trial, the drugs were in the suitcases' handles. Nesbeth met the profile of a courier, and there was a clear basis for the jury to reject her claim that she did not know she was bringing drugs into the country.

The Probation Department recommended a below-guidelines sentence of twenty-four months, followed by three years of supervised release, because she was a first-time offender, was enrolled in college, was employed, had otherwise lived a law-abiding life, and was at a low risk of recidivism.

Nesbeth, who was twenty years old when convicted, was born in Kingston, Jamaica. Her mother had left her in Jamaica to be raised by her father; in 2008, when she was thirteen, she joined her mother in the United States. She now lived with her mother in New Haven, Connecticut. She became a U.S. citizen and had been enrolled in college since 2013. She had always been single and did not have any children. She helped support herself as a nail technician at a children's spa. Between September 2012 and June 2013, she worked as a counselor at a facility that provided services to children in lower-income areas, and during the summers of 2010 through 2012, she held seasonal employment as a parks maintenance worker.

Not surprisingly, Nesbeth's mother, who was a home care attendant, was "shocked" by her daughter's arrest and conviction because it was "completely out of character." She described her daughter as "an 'excellent' person, who is quiet, nice, caring, and who is both very loving and very loved." The mother also related "that the defendant worries about her future, as she had planned to be a school principal."

In the United States, Nesbeth was raised under lower-income circumstances, and her family had for a time required food stamps. As for her education, she anticipated graduating from Southern Connecticut State University in 2017. The presentence report stated that "[s]he was originally studying education" but "due to the instant conviction is now studying sociology." Moreover, she owed several thousand dollars in student loans. She reported no illegal drug use, and to her mother's knowledge her daughter had "never used illegal drugs, consumed alcohol, or required substance abuse treatment."

Concerned about possible collateral consequences Nesbeth might face, I had requested the Probation Department, as well as her attorney and the government's prosecutor, to advise me of the federal collateral consequences she would likely encounter because of her felony drug conviction. I was astounded by what they reported.

- She would be ineligible for grants, loans, and work assistance for a period of two years—the duration of her college career.
- For a period of one year, she would be ineligible "for the issuance of any grant, contract, loan, professional license, or commercial license provided by an agency of or appropriated by funds of the United States."
- She and her household may be denied admission to federally assisted housing for a "reasonable time."
- She would be ineligible for food stamps.
- She would not be issued a passport during supervised re-

lease; thus, she could not visit her father, grandmother, and extended family in Jamaica.

- She would have her driver's license suspended or revoked for a period of "at least six months."
- She would likely be subject to a criminal background check for any employment in under-eighteen-year-old childcare services, and her drug conviction may therefore be grounds for denying such employment.
- She could not work in a foreign student exchange program sponsored by the Department of State.

The list went on and on: a felony conviction permanently barred Nesbeth from working for a manufacturer, distributor, dispenser, or reverse dispenser of controlled substances; barred employment with private transportation companies transporting prisoners or hazardous materials and as an airport security screener or baggage handler, a flight crew member, and a customs broker; barred employment for a hospice if the conviction was within three years and the applicant would have contact with patient records; and barred employment in an FDIC-insured depository institution within ten years of conviction.

A felony conviction would also permanently bar her from receiving disaster relief and possessing, selling, shipping, or receiving a lawful firearm in both interstate and foreign commerce; nor could a convicted felon adopt a child or serve as a foster parent for five years.

Another federal statute bars those convicted of a felony in federal and state courts "from serving as either a grand juror or a petit juror unless the person's civil rights have been restored, which can only be achieved through a pardon," and they may be precluded from enlisting in the armed forces or be ineligible for working in a labor organization or for an employee benefits plan.

As if the federal preclusions were not enough, Nesbeth would also be subject to Connecticut laws, where she resided. Thus, she would not be allowed to vote in Connecticut elections until her term of supervised release had expired, could not serve on a jury for seven years, would be disqualified from receiving a teaching certificate for five years, and may be ineligible for Connecticut public housing.

If she resided in New York, she would be subject to comparable restrictions, and if she were a bingo devotee, she could not even receive a bingo operator's license.

I weighed these collateral consequences and did not send Chevelle Nesbeth to jail. I sentenced her, instead, to one year of probation, with two special conditions: six months of home confinement and one hundred hours of community service.

In the more than two decades I have been on the bench, no judge had ever formally addressed the devastating statutory collateral consequences facing an individual trying to reintegrate into society once released from prison or jail. I wrote, therefore, that henceforth it should be "the obligation of both the defense lawyer and the prosecutors, as well as the Probation Department in the preparation of its Presentence Report, to assess and apprise the court, prior to sentencing, of the likely collateral consequences facing a convicted defendant."

I concluded my opinion with the following observation:

> While consideration of the collateral consequences a convicted felon must face should be part of a sentencing judge's calculus in arriving at a just punishment, it does nothing, of course, to mitigate the fact that those consequences will still attach. It is for Congress and the states' legislatures to determine whether the plethora of

post-sentence punishments imposed upon felons is truly
warranted, and to take a hard look at whether they do
the country more harm than good.[2]

My *Nesbeth* decision garnered a lot of press. True to form, the
New York Post published an editorial headlined, "Brooklyn Judge
Attempts to Rewrite Laws with an Outrageous Wrist-Slap for
Drug Felon."[3] But, happily, other publications took a different
view. A front-page *New York Times* article, bearing the headline
"U.S. Judge's Striking Move in Felony Drug Case: Probation, Not
Prison," began by reporting: "A federal judge in Brooklyn, in an
extraordinary opinion . . . that calls for courts to pay closer attention to how felony convictions affect people's lives sentenced a
woman in a drug case to probation rather than prison, saying that
the collateral consequences she would face as a felon were punishment enough."[4]

More major publications followed suit. A lengthy article in *The
Atlantic* began by stating: "Last week, a federal judge in Brooklyn issued a ruling that sent a small shockwave through the criminal justice world."[5] A few months later, Lincoln Caplan, a senior
research scholar at Yale Law School, wrote a piece for the *New Yorker*
about the opinion, commenting that "federal judges throughout the
country have been sending it to one another as a cutting-edge view
on an important issue in sentencing." In it he referenced Jeremy
Travis, the criminal justice scholar who had written that "legislatures have often adopted collateral consequences in unaccount-
able ways: 'as riders to other, major pieces of legislation,' which are
'given scant attention.'" Travis called them "invisible ingredients in
the legislative menu of criminal sanctions" (a phrase that inspired
a Sentencing Project book on the topic of collateral consequences
entitled *Invisible Punishment*).

The *New Yorker* article concluded,

The judge made clear why the severity of collateral consequences—authorizing discrimination in education, employment, housing, and many other basic elements of American life—means that anyone convicted of a felony is likely to face an arduous future. This predicament has been called modern civil death, social exclusion, and internal exile. Whatever it is called, its vast array of penalties kicks in automatically with a conviction, defying the supposedly bedrock principle of American law that the punishment must fit the crime.[6]

And I was particularly pleased with the headline of a praiseworthy article in *Slate*: "In a Remarkable Decision, Federal Judge Lays Out All the Ways Our Justice System Hurts Ex-Cons."[7]

In wrapping up this book, I was happy to read an article written a few years ago for the conservative Heritage Foundation, which reinforced my belief that the need to address our collateral consequences problem crosses ideological lines. It was written by John Malcolm, vice president of the Institute for Constitutional Government and director of the Heritage Foundation's Center for Legal and Judicial Studies, who wrote,

> Some collateral consequences—such as prohibitions against violent felons possessing a firearm or restrictions against pedophiles operating a day-care center—are clearly warranted. But others do not seem grounded in the interests of public safety. Rather, they seem designed primarily to continue punishing people who have already served their sentences.
>
> Such restrictions can severely hamper an ex-offender's ability to get a job or a professional license. . . . Of the

tens of thousands of identified collateral consequences on the books, 60–70 percent are employment-related, despite the fact that unemployment is a top predictor of recidivism. . . .

It is not in anyone's best interests to consign ex-offenders to a permanent second-class status. Doing so will only lead to wasted lives, ruined families and more crime.[8]

After *Nesbeth*, there has been some movement among the states to address collateral consequences, but hardly enough. Twelve have passed "Clean Slate Initiative" laws, which generally either expunge or seal misdemeanor or low-level felony offenses after a period of years. Although limited to misdemeanors and low-level felonies, this "record relief" nonetheless is important because for those convicted of these lesser crimes, it reduces the negative effect of a criminal record for housing and employment. However, this relief can take up to eight years to kick in, which means that many formerly incarcerated people have no relief when they most need it—when they first leave prison.[9]

In 2022, twenty states commendably enacted laws limiting consideration of criminal records in regulating employment and granting occupational licenses.[10] Additionally, between 2015 and 2021, twenty-two states and the District of Columbia enacted laws granting voting rights for formerly incarcerated people.[11] But more must be done.

A number of federal consequences are particularly ludicrous. For example, anyone who commits a controlled substance offense, any crime of violence, or even a motor vehicle offense, is ineligible for a farm-related commercial driver's license. Moreover, as the Second Circuit Court of Appeals has held, the federal courts have no power to expunge records of a valid conviction. Thus, as the Brennan Center reports, "the federal system has few ways to protect criminal records."[12]

A Clean Slate Initiative bill is pending before Congress, but its passage is problematic.[13] Some agencies, however, have acted, such as the Small Business Administration, which has eliminated ineligibility for participation in its veteran-owned small business development program.[14] And in 2022 the Biden administration announced that it would pardon all prior federal offenders of simple possession of marijuana, which President Biden described as necessary to "relieve the collateral consequences arising from these convictions."[15] These tiny steps are in the right direction, but are obviously just a drop in the bucket.

EPILOGUE

The cases I have written about document the newfound discretion given to me by the First Step Act's catchall clause. But that clause also allows a district judge to correct egregiously imposed mandatory minimum sentences that bear no rational correlation to the crimes of conviction. I have thought about a few good examples.

When James Sessoms brought his compassionate release motion to me, he had been serving a sentence of thirty-five years, over 70% of which was attributable to the prosecutorial practice known as "stacking." If not for that, he would have been sentenced to seventeen years and have then been a free man.

In 2006, Sessoms had been tried and convicted by a jury for several crimes—none involving the loss of life—before my late colleague Judge David Trager. Two crimes involved a firearm associated with a crime committed on the same day—one for use and the other for possession. Under the law at that time, the sentence for the second firearm charge carried a mandatory minimum of twenty-five years to be tacked on to the other charges. At the sentencing, Judge

Trager was critical of this stacking. He stated that "[a]lthough Mr. Sessoms deserves a substantial sentence, I don't think 35 years is appropriate. But right now I have no discretion here." He then adjourned the sentence to allow for the possibility that pending legislation might mitigate that harsh result.

Judge Trager passed away before he sentenced Sessoms, and the case was reassigned to me. I had no choice but to impose the thirty-five-year mandatory minimum that the law required at the time. In 1993, the Supreme Court had upheld the validity of the statute that required twenty-five years to be added for "a second or subsequent conviction," even if part of the same underlying crimes were contained in a single indictment. As Justice Stevens presciently observed in dissent, this gave prosecutors "considerable discretion in deciding how many . . . offenses to charge in relation to a criminal transaction or series of transactions."[1] Hence, this practice of stacking led to Sessoms's draconian sentence.

Congress finally recognized the manifest unfairness of that statute in the First Step Act by eliminating this twenty-five-year mandatory penalty; however, in what may well have been a compromise for those who opposed this humane sentencing reform, it provided that this change of law would not apply retroactively.

I granted Sessoms compassionate relief and released him from jail. It just seemed unfair to me that some convicted felons would have twenty-five years removed from their sentences, while others would remain victimized by this onerous statute because the law was not made retroactive. However, one thing was perfectly clear: if not for the discretion now vested in me by the First Step Act to revisit excessive sentences, James Sessoms might still be in jail.[2]

Another case that caught my attention was a recent one from the Southern District of Indiana, where the district judge granted compassionate release to an inmate who had received a life sentence and had been incarcerated for a simple drug offense for more than fourteen years because he had been designated as a career offender.[3] Under current sentencing guidelines, he would not have received either this designation or a life sentence. If not for the First Step Act, he would not have been released.

And closer to home, an even more recent decision, rendered on January 19, 2024, by former chief judge Colleen McMahon of the Southern District of New York, abrogated a previously imposed absurd mandatory minimum sentence. Judge McMahon—who is not known as a soft sentencer—had previously sentenced James Cromitie to a mandatory minimum of twenty-five years, but she now reduced his sentence after he had served fifteen years "to time served plus 90 days." She explained that before the enactment of the First Step Act she had no discretion but to impose the mandatory minimum; but the circumstances underlying that sentence warranted the granting of his compassionate release motion.

Cromitie was the victim of a manufactured "sting" operation by the government and, as explained by Judge McMahon, "was sentenced for participating in a fictitious plot to do things that he could never have dreamed up on his own, and that were never going to happen." The "plot" that triggered the twenty-five-year mandatory minimum was "a conspiracy to shoot down military aircraft with phony 'stinger missiles' created by the government." But as Judge McMahon stated, "Nothing could be more certain than the fact that Cromitie and his codefendants could not have devised on their own a crime involving missiles that would have warranted the twenty-five-year sentence the court was forced to impose."

In releasing Cromitie after he had served fifteen years for this phony crime, Judge McMahon was highly critical of the "government's questionable decision" to send "a villain" to "troll among the poorest and weakest of men for 'terrorists' who might prove susceptible to an offer of much-needed cash in exchange for committing a faux crime."[4]

* * *

The six cases I have written about in this book make for dramatic reading. But I have tried to use them also as vehicles for raising many issues that merit serious thought and debate about our justice system, in addition to highlighting the failure of the states to embrace the First Step Act and the counterintuitive post-release collateral consequences.

Woven throughout are many other issues that trouble me, such as our ongoing mass incarceration problem; the excessively lengthy sentences we mete out; the efficacy of the death penalty; our schizoid gun and drug laws; the plethora of congressionally imposed mandatory minimums; the emotional, but often irrational, sentences imposed on those convicted of sex crimes, particularly crimes involving children; the "trial tax" prosecutors impose on a defendant's constitutional right to trial; the glut of wrongful convictions; the grant of absolute immunity for prosecutorial misconduct: the failure to hold prosecutors accountable for their intentional misdeeds: the overly punitive nature of sentences on the juvenile criminal; our imprisonment of the aged, often demented, inmate; the failure of our Supreme Court justices to embrace the same canons of ethics adhered to by every other federal court judge; and the proliferation of death threats against our nation's judges.

These are not easy issues and there are no simple answers or solutions. But we must ween ourselves from the simplistic lay public cliché that "if you do the crime, you do the time," and we must intelligently and rationally assess and address these issues.

I hope this book will lead to a greater public awareness of some of the complexities and difficulties facing all those tasked with providing a more just and humane criminal legal system.

CODA

We, the undersigned, come to criminal justice reform from divergent perspectives. While the prosecutor and the defense attorney are adversaries in criminal proceedings, we are often aligned in promoting a justice system that is grounded in fairness, equity, compassion, and fiscal responsibility. Nowhere are those values more significantly challenged than in our nation's approach to sentencing.

The United States has the highest incarceration rate in the world. This is not because we are a nation of criminals. It is because of a long-standing national obsession over many years with increasingly harsh sentences that often lock people in prison for decades—if not longer—without regard to the detrimental impact on communities, individuals, and society itself.

There is mounting evidence that people who have served many years behind bars can be released and allowed to return to their family and community with limited impact on public safety. It is virtually impossible at the time of sentencing to anticipate an individual's capacity for change, and individuals who have "aged out" of criminal behavior pose a very low risk of committing new crimes. Additionally, data establishes that long sentences have no meaningful effect on crime deterrence and the cost of imprisoning aging individuals is diverting precious resources that could be used for crime reduction and community safety and well-being initiatives. For these reasons, there is an urgent need to enact reforms that create a mechanism to review past lengthy prison sentences.

A small step in that direction was taken in 2018, when the First Step Act provided an avenue for incarcerated federal prisoners to seek judicial review of harsh sentences in some limited circumstances. Judges drive how this reform plays out in practice.

In *A Second Chance*, United States District Judge Frederic Block has provided an important account of the vast power judges possess in determining an individual's length of incarceration—both at the time of sentencing and now, under the First Step Act, in responding to requests for review of past sentences. Judge Block has invited the reader to don the robes of a judge and sit beside him as he describes the complex factors that are weighed in deciding whether to give a person a chance at freedom. This is not a legal treatise or a judicial memoir. Rather it is a close look at the real-life situations that judges encounter every day and the human implications of the decisions they make.

A Second Chance does a lot more than merely transport the reader into the courtroom to see these stories unfold. Judge Block has described the origins of the First Step Act, a bipartisan effort that produced one of the most significant federal criminal legal reforms in recent years. He also has recounted systemic problems throughout the United States that promote injustice. But Judge Block does not speak to these issues from some lofty plain, he illustrates them through the profiles of actual cases and injustices. From Chevelle Nesbeth, a twenty-year-old woman convicted of a first nonviolent offense facing life-altering collateral consequences, to Steven May, a thirty-seven-year-old defendant sentenced effectively to life without parole for a crime he may not have committed, to Jabbar Collins who spent sixteen years in prison for a wrongful conviction because witnesses lied at his trial, Judge Block confronts the stark reality of a system sorely in need of reform.

From his unique perch as a sitting judge, Judge Block has compellingly made the case for reform legislation to revisit past extreme sentences throughout the nation. He aptly notes that the vast majority of individuals behind bars are in state, and not federal, custody, while the First Step Act only applies to federal sentences. These avenues for resentencing—on both the federal and state levels—are vital if the United States is to end mass incarceration. We join Judge Block in his urgent call for change and his recognition that a system of justice must embrace the need for second chances.

Miriam Krinsky
former prosecutor and
executive director of Fair
and Just Prosecution

Norman L. Reimer
defense attorney and former
executive director of National
Association of Criminal
Defense Lawyers (2006–2021)

AUTHOR'S NOTE

I have taken the liberty of borrowing from some of the sections I had written twelve years ago in my book *Disrobed: An Inside Look at the Life and Work of a Federal Trial Judge*, where that material illustrates points being made in this volume about the death penalty, our drug laws, and our gun laws. These sections have been brought current. I have also retold from the book some of the colorful stories from my Peter Gotti trial, as well as some material from my book *Crimes and Punishments*. Finally, mindful that the contents of presentence reports should not be disclosed other than what a sentencing judge relies upon in rendering the sentence, counsel for Russo, Amuso, and Birkett have advised me that their clients had no objections to the disclosure of the contents of their presentence reports.

ACKNOWLEDGMENTS

It all started with Burt Neuborne, the distinguished Professor of Civil Liberties at New York University School of Law and founding legal director of the Brennan Center for Justice. Burt knew that The New Press had published Michelle Alexander's acclaimed *The New Jim Crow* and suggested to Diane Wachtell, the executive director and co-founder of The New Press, that my book might be of interest. I had a high regard for The New Press because it filled a void that the conventional commercial presses often overlook—the importance of publishing books of social, economic. and political significance and critiques of our criminal legal system.

Diane was indeed interested and suggested expanding my argument in favor of the First Step Act to a call for the states to give their judges the same power the act gave to federal district judges—the discretion to reconsider previously imposed sentences and to give worthy prisoners a "second chance" to reclaim their lives.

The staff of The New Press also deserves recognition. They were meticulous in making the book error free and, hopefully, factually correct. Their support and belief in its value was of great comfort to me. A special thanks go to the folks who designed the terrific jacket.

My wife, Betsy, was a good sport and read the several iterations as they were being written. She offered helpful constructive comments and encouraged me to get to the finish line. Her children, Debbie and Tina, whom I affectionately claim as my children as well, were of moral support, as were their husbands, George and Trevor.

My colleagues Judges Raymond Dearie and Brian Cogan encouraged me to write the book, and Judge Dearie sent me the article from the *New York Times* about the Donnell Drinks case and the inappropriate sentences meted out to teenagers. Our collective friend Paul Bergman also took an interest in what I was doing and sent me the *New York Times* article about aging, demented prisoners.

Special thanks go to my law clerks Kyle Bigley, Josh Howard, and Ty Cone. Their excellent research in drafting proposed decisions for my consideration for our compassionate release motions triggered my decision to write the book. Kyle merits a particular shout-out for compiling the footnotes. In addition, Daniella Sapone, Andrew Kasses, Marcus Villanueva, and Mitch Krupnik, my 2023 summer interns, did some preliminary research which helped me conceptualize the arc of the book.

I also want to thank the court's clerk and case manager Mike Innelli for keeping my judicial foot to the pedal so that there would be no slippage in the discharge of my judicial responsibilities while I was writing the book.

Many lawyer friends read the book as it was unfolding. Dane Butswinkas came up with the suspenseful idea of telling the stories of the compassionate release candidates in the first part of the book, and then telling the reader what I decided in the third part—after explained the First Step Act in between. Norman Reimer, the former executive director of the National Association of Criminal Defense Lawyers (NACDL), the country's leading Criminal Defense Bar, offered numerous invaluable constructive suggestions. Gary Villanueva, Mimi and Steve Hyman, Frank and Sunny Velie, John Horan, Bob and Abbie Fink, Steve Zissou, Matt Giffuni, and Michael Padden were also very helpful. And last, but hardly least, my colleague the venerable Judge I. Leo Glaser, who still functions as an active district court judge, even though he is ten years older than I am, read large portions of the book as it was being written and encouraged me to finish it.

Friends who are not lawyers also deserve my thanks. Marci and Ron Holzer, Sean Dana, Jerry Krystopf, and Carlos Valentin come readily to mind. And special thanks go to my friend Ed Lederman, a highly acclaimed photographer, for the ridiculous amount of time he took for my picture to make it perfect.

Finally, I want to thank Stephen May's parents for contacting me and sending me the letters from juror #1 and the late Dr. Gold's wife, as well as the transcript of the hearing before the Arizona Clemency Board. I was naturally saddened when they shared with me their heart-wrenching angst in dealing with the reality that their son will probably die in prison.

NOTES

Introduction

1. Federal Bureau of Prisons, "First Step Act," www.bop.gov/inmates /fsa/.

2. *Vox* reported in 2016 that the United States had 4% of the world's population but 22% of the world's prison population. German Lopez, "Mass Incarceration in America, Explained in 22 Maps and Charts," *Vox*, October 11, 2016, www.vox.com/2015/7/13/8913297/mass-incarceration -maps-charts.

3. Wendy Sawyer and Peter Wagner, "Mass Incarceration: The Whole Pie 2023," *Prison Policy Initiative*, March 14, 2023, www.prisonpolicy.org /reports/pie2023.html.

4. Liz Benecchi, "Recidivism Imprisons American Progress," *Harvard Political Review*, August 8, 2021, harvardpolitics.com/recidivism -american-progress.

5. Peter Wagner and Bernadette Rabuy, "Following the Money of Mass Incarceration," *Prison Policy Initiative*, January 25, 2017, www.prisonpolicy .org/reports/money.html.

6. Benecchi, "Recidivism."

7. Ashley Nellis and Liz Komar, "The First Step Act: Ending Mass Incarceration in Federal Prisons," The Sentencing Project, August 22, 2023, www.sentencingproject.org/policy-brief/the-first-step-act-ending -mass-incarceration-in-federal-prisons.

8. The quotes and statistics from this paragraph are drawn from Sawyer and Wagner, "Mass Incarceration."

9. Sawyer and Wagner, "Mass Incarceration"; California Penal Code §1170(d) permits defendants who were under eighteen years at the time of their crime, sentenced to life without the possibility of parole, and have been incarcerated for at least fifteen years to apply to their sentencing court for recall and resentencing. Pennsylvania permits terminally ill or medically incapacitated prisoners to apply directly to their sentencing court for release on compassionate grounds. Families Against Mandatory Minimums: FAMM, "Compassionate Release: Pennsylvania," famm .org/wp-content/uploads/PennsylvaniaFinal.pdf. Ohio's "Judicial Release" statute permits inmates sentenced to nonmandatory sentences to apply for early release, including on medical grounds. Families Against Mandatory Minimums: FAMM, "Compassionate Release: Ohio," famm.org/wp-content/uploads/OhioFinal.pdf. The District of Columbia's Second Look Amendment Act of 2019 allows people who committed a crime before they were twenty-five to petition the court for resentencing if they have served fifteen years of their sentence. Public Defender Service for the District of Columbia, "The New Law: The Second Look Amendment Act," www .pdsdc.org/resources/client-resources/second-look-amendment. In 2023, Colorado amended its criminal code to permit defendants who were "sentenced to 24 years or more under the state's 'habitual offender' statute and who have served at least ten years" to petition courts for sentence modification. Nicole D. Porter, "Top Trends in Criminal Legal Reform, 2023," The Sentencing Project, December 20, 2023, www.sentencingproject.org /publications/top-trends-in-criminal-legal-reform-2023/. New Jersey Rule 3:21-10(b)(2) allows prisoners to petition for direct relief in court because of the illness or infirmity of the defendant. State v. Chavies, 247 N.J. 245, 249 (2021). Current reporting on state-by-state sentencing reform comes from Families Against Mandatory Minimums, which tracks state compassionate release procedures and resentencing statutes. Families Against Mandatory Minimums: FAMM, famm.org.

10. New York City Bar Association, "The Second Chance Amendment: Legislative Proposal," www.nycbar.org/reports/the-second-chance-amendment-legislative-proposal/.

11. Frank E. Lockwood, "Cotton Opposes Bill to Trim Prison Terms, Calls It Too Lenient," *Arkansas Democrat Gazette*, December 2, 2018, www.arkansasonline.com/news/2018/dec/02/cotton-opposes-bill-to-trim-prison-term.

12. Pence and DeSantis are quoted in Chris Stein, "Struggling DeSantis and Pence Attack Criminal Justice Law They Championed," *Guardian*, July 23, 2023.

13. Pulsifer v. United States, 601 U. S. ____ (2024) (Gorsuch, J., dissenting) (internal quotations omitted).

14. National Center for Drug Abuse Statistics, "Drug Related Crime Statistics," drugabusestatistics.org/drug-related-crime-statistics/#:~:text=46%25%20of%20prisoners%20in%20federal,serving%20time%20for%20drug%20offenses.

15. Statistic reported in Drug Policy Alliance, "The Drug War, Mass Incarceration and Race," June 2015.

16. Jorge Renaud, "Grading the Parole Release Systems of All 50 States," *Prison Policy Initiative*, February 26, 2019, www.prisonpolicy.org/reports/grading_parole.html.

1. Justin Volpe

1. The quotations and facts in the following discussion are taken from Judge Nickerson's opinion in United States v. Volpe, 78 F. Supp. 2d 76 (E.D.N.Y. 1999).

2. *New York Daily News*, "5 Cops Face Trial in Louima Attack," March 28, 1999, www.nydailynews.com/1999/03/28/5-cops-face-trial-in-louima-attack/.

3. Timothy Williams, "Thousands Protest Brutality in Louima Case," *Associated Press*, August 30, 1997, www.southcoasttoday.com/story/news/nation-world/1997/08/30/thousands-protest-brutality-in-louima/50596356007/.

4. Joseph P. Fried, "Volpe Sentenced to a 30-Year Term in Louima Torture," *New York Times*, December 14, 1999.

5. United States v. Volpe, 224 F.3d 72 (2d Cir. 2000).

6. Murray Weiss, "Mom: Volpe's Term Longer Than Cop Killer's," *New York Post*, December 15, 1999.

7. *BBC News*, "New York Pays for Police Brutality," July 13, 2001, web .archive.org/web/20140104020256/http://news.bbc.co.uk/2/hi/americas /1436538.stm.

8. Associated Press, "N.Y. Police Victim Changes His Pain to Hope for Haiti," February 26, 2003, web.archive.org/web/20140106040131 /http://www.sptimes.com/2003/02/26/news_pf/Worldandnation /NY_police_victim_chan.shtml.

9. Sewell Chan, "The Abner Louima Case, 10 Years Later," *New York Times*, August 9, 2007.

10. Louima's quotations in this and the following paragraph are taken from Jack Morphet and Steve Janoski, "Abner Louima Says He Forgives Justin Volpe—But Will Never Forget Brutal Assault After Ex-cop Is Released Early from Prison," *New York Post*, June 13, 2023.

11. Zack Beauchamp, "What the Police Really Believe," *Vox*, July 7, 2020.

2. Sherwin Birkett

1. Britannica.com, "Racketeer Influenced and Corrupt Organizations Act."

2. George S. Roukis and Bruche H. Charnov, "RICO (Racketeer Influenced and Corrupt Organizations Act) Statute—Implications for Organized Labor," *Labor Law Journal*, 36, no. 5 (May 1985): 281–91.

3. Citations for the above discussion are available in my article Frederic Block, "Racism's Hidden History in the War on Drugs," *HuffPost*, January 3, 2013.

4. Kathleen Sandy, "The Discrimination Inherent in America's Drug War: Hidden Racism Revealed by Examining the Hysteria over Crack," *Alabama Law Review* 54, no. 2 (2003): 665.

5. Block, "Racism's Hidden History."

6. National Survey on Drug Use and Health, "Table 1.1A: Types of Illicit Drug Use in Lifetime, Past Year, and Past Month: Among People Aged 12 or Older; Numbers in Thousands, 2021 and 2022," www.samhsa .gov/data/sites/default/files/reports/rpt42728/NSDUHDetailedTabs2022 /NSDUHDetailedTabs2022/NSDUHDetTabsSect1pe2022.htm.

7. National Center for Drug Abuse Statistics, "Marijuana Addiction: Rates and Usage Statistics," drugabusestatistics.org/marijuana-addiction /#:~:text=Among%2012th%20graders%2C%206%25%20continue,in%20 16%20high%20school%20seniors.

8. National Conference of State Legislatures, "State Medical Cannabis Laws," www.ncsl.org/health/state-medical-cannabis-laws#:~:text=Non %2DMedical%2FAdult%2DUse,medical%20adult%20(recreational)%20 use.

9. Birkett v. United States, No. 90 CR 1063 (SJ), 2009 WL 10655836 (E.D.N.Y. June 1, 2009).

10. My decision granting Moore's sentence reduction is contained in the consolidated opinion, United States v. Russo, 643 F. Supp. 3d 325 (E.D.N.Y. 2022).

3. Joe Smith

1. United States Sentencing Commission, "Quick Facts: Child Pornography Offenders Fiscal Year 2020," www.ussc.gov/sites/default/files/pdf /research-and-publications/quick-facts/Child_Pornography_FY20.pdf.

5. The Mafia Cases: Vittorio "Little Vic" Amuso

1. Congress makes this statement in 18 U.S.C. §922(q).

2. Giffords Law Center, "Assault Weapons," giffords.org/lawcenter /gun-laws/policy-areas/hardware-ammunition/assault-weapons /#:~:text=Ten%20states%20(California%2C%20Connecticut%2C,and% 20transfer%20of%20assault%20weapons.

3. Giffords Law Center, "Bulk Gun Purchases," giffords.org/lawcenter /gun-laws/policy-areas/crime-guns/bulk-gun-purchases/#:~:text=Five%20

states%20(California%2C%20Connecticut%2C,individuals%20may%20 purchase%20each%20month.

4. Federal law prohibits licensed firearms dealers from selling or delivering a handgun to any person the dealer has reasonable cause to believe is under age twenty-one and unlicensed persons from selling, delivering, or transferring a handgun to any person the "transferor knows or has reasonable cause to believe is under age 18, with certain exceptions." Giffords Law Center, "Minimum Age to Purchase and Possess," giffords.org/lawcenter /gun-laws/policy-areas/who-can-have-a-gun/minimum-age.

5. "There is no minimum age to possess rifles and shotguns in North Carolina." Giffords Law Center, "Minimum Age to Purchase and Possess in North Carolina," giffords.org/lawcenter/state-laws/minimum-age-to -purchase-possess-in-north-carolina.

6. National Rifle Association, Institute for Legislative Action, "Guide to the Interstate Transportation of Firearms," January 1, 2015, www.nraila .org/articles/20150101/guide-to-the-interstate-transportation.

7. Lydia Saad, "What Percentage of Americans Own Guns?" Gallup, November 13, 2020, news.gallup.com/poll/264932/percentage-americans -own-guns.aspx.

8. Ray Sanchez, Miguel Marquez, and Sarah Boxer, "A Nation Rocked by Mass Shootings Goes on an Extended Gun-Buying Run," *CNN*, April 22, 2023, www.cnn.com/2023/04/22/us/united-states-rising-gun -sales/index.html.

9. Federal Bureau of Investigation, "NICS Firearm Background Checks: Month/Year," www.fbi.gov/file-repository/nics_firearm_checks_ -_month_year.pdf.

10. World Population Review, "Gun Deaths by Country 2023," world-populationreview.com/country-rankings/gun-deaths-by-country.

11. Everytown Research and Policy, "The US Gun Homicide Rate Is 26 Times That of Other High-Income Countries," everytownresearch .org/graph/the-u-s-gun-homicide-rate-is-26-times-that-of-other-high -income-countries.

12. Bob Herbert, "The American Way," *New York Times*, April 13, 2009.

13. Bruce Hoffman and Jacob Ware, "Opinion: Is the US on the Brink of Another Civil War?," CNN, March 16, 2024, www.cnn.com/2024/03/16 /opinions/us-brink-of-civil-war-hoffman-ware/index.html.

14. Kiara Alfonseca, "There Have Been More Mass Shootings Than Days in 2023, Database Shows," *ABC News*, September 5, 2023, abc7news .com/there-have-been-more-mass-shootings-than-days-in-2023-database -shows/13030909.

15. Gun Violence Archive, "Gun Violence Archive 2023," www .gunviolencearchive.org.

16. Martie Bowser, "7 Countries with Travel Bans Against the US," *Miami Herald*, May 1, 2023, www.miamiherald.com/detour/article274840151 .html.

6. The Mafia Cases: Anthony "Gaspipe" Casso

1. Priscilla DeGregory, Larry Celona, and Tamar Lapin, "Ex-Lucchese Underboss Anthony 'Gaspipe' Casso Dies After Getting COVID-19 in Prison," *New York Post*, December 16, 2020.

2. At their peak in the mid-1990s, cooperation rates hovered around 20%, but in recent years they have come down to around 10%. Jessica A. Roth, Anna D. Vaynman, and Steven D. Penrod, "Why Criminal Defendants Cooperate: The Defense Attorney's Perspective," *Northwestern University Law Review* 117, no. 5 (2023): 1361–62.

3. Jerry Capeci and Tom Robbins, *Mob Boss: The First Boss to Turn Government Witness* (New York: St. Martin's Press, 2015), 443.

4. My opinion is available at United States v. Casso, 9 F. Supp. 2d 199 (E.D.N.Y. 1998).

5. Vera Bergengruen, "Trump Attacks on Prosecutors and Judges Heighten Security Concerns," *Time*, August 15, 2023, time.com/6303523 /trump-prosecutors-violent-threats.

6. Nina Totenberg, "An Attacker Killed a Judge's Son. Now She Wants to Protect Other Families," NPR, November 20, 2020, www.npr.org /2020/11/20/936717194/a-judge-watched-her-son-die-now-she-wants -to-protect-other-judicial-families.

7. *Ibid.*

8. Nate Raymond and Patricia Zengerie, "Judicial Security Measure Clears U.S. Congress as Part of Defense Bill," Reuters, December 15, 2022.

9. Totenberg, "An Attacker Killed."

10. Jerry Markon, "Court Officials Turn to Guards, Identity Shields, Weapons to Handle New Threats," *Washington Post*, May 25, 2009.

11. Dennis Romero and Lindsay Good, "Man Who Leaped at Judge Charged with Attempted Murder in Nevada Courtroom Attack," *NBC News*, January 30, 2024, www.nbcnews.com/news/us-news/man-leaped -judge-charged-attempted-murder-nevada-courtroom-attack-rcna133149.

12. Bergengruen, "Trump Attacks."

13. Emily Olson, "A Texas Woman Is Charged with Threatening the Judge Overseeing Trump's Jan. 6 Trial," NPR, August 17, 2023, www .npr.org/2023/08/17/1194362551/tanya-chutkan-judge-threats-trump -insurrection-trial-shry.

14. American Bar Association, "As Threats Intensify, Judges Urge Colleagues to Speak Out," August 2019, www.americanbar.org/news/abanews /aba-news-archives/2019/08/as-threats-intensify-judges-urge/.

15. Joseph Tanfani, Peter Eisler, and Ned Parker, "Exclusive: Threats to U.S. Federal Judges Double Since 2021, Driven by Politics," Reuters, February 13, 2024.

16. Greco v. City of New York, No. 22CV5109FBVMS, 2023 WL 5024720 (E.D.N.Y. Aug. 8, 2023).

7. The First Step Act

1. The discussion and quotes in the following paragraph are drawn from German Lopez, "Trump's Criminal Justice Policy, Explained," *Vox*, September 11, 2020, www.vox.com/2020-presidential-election/21418911 /donald-trump-crime-criminal-justice-policy-record.

2. Trump's quote from *The America We Deserve* is in Lopez, "Trump's Criminal Justice Policy, Explained."

3. Associated Press, "The Latest: Trump Hails Passage of Criminal Justice Bill," December 19, 2018, apnews.com/article/af276b3dfa 8548f0b1f9992e60bb59f0; Trump White House, "President Donald J. Trump Secures Landmark Legislation to Make Our Federal Justice System Fairer and Our Communities Safer," December 21, 2018, trump-whitehouse.archives.gov/briefings-statements/president-donald-j-trump -secures-landmark-legislation-to-make-our-federal-justice-system-fairer -and-our-communities-safer.

4. Barkow is quoted in Lopez, "Trump's Criminal Justice Policy, Explained."

5. Maggie Haberman, "Pardon Recipients Seek to Sell Trump on His Own Sentencing Law," *New York Times*, November 18, 2023.

6. Michael Romano, "How Biden Can Tackle Mass Incarceration," *New York Times*, December 29, 2023.

7. Nicholas Fandos, "Senate Passes Bipartisan Criminal Justice Bill," *New York Times*, December 18, 2018.

8. Jill Colvin and Colleen Long, "Kushner Pardon Revives 'Loathsome' Tale of Tax Evasion, Sex," Associated Press, apnews.com /article/donald-trump-charles-kushner-new-jersey-elections-crime -0155d15fa31108fd2c0e6360a3b597dd#:~:text=%E2%80%9CWhen%20 you're%20on%20the,and%20deserve%20a%20second%20chance.

9. Colvin and Long, "Kushner Pardon Revives 'Loathsome' Tale of Tax Evasion, Sex."

10. Trump White House, "Statement from the Press Secretary Regarding Executive Grants of Clemency," December 23, 2020, trumpwhitehouse .archives.gov/briefings-statements/statement-press-secretary-regarding -executive-grants-clemency-122320.

11. Colvin and Long, "Kushner Pardon."

12. Prison to Employment Connection, "Do You Know?," prison2ec .org/facts/#:~:text=Formerly%20incarcerated%20persons%20who%20 maintained,who%20did%20not%20maintain%20employment.

13. Jay Inslee, "How Norwegian Prisons Prepare Inmates to Become Better Neighbors," *Medium*, September 22, 2022, medium.com/wagovernor

232 NOTES

/how-norwegian-prisons-prepare-inmates-to-become-better-neighbors
-534409a90f33.

14. United States Sentencing Commission, "Report to the Congress:
Mandatory Minimum Penalties in the Federal Criminal Justice System," October 2011, D-7, www.ussc.gov/sites/default/files/pdf/news
/congressional-testimony-and-reports/mandatory-minimum-penalties
/20111031-rtc-pdf/Appendix_D.pdf.

15. Chapman v. United States, 500 U.S. 453 (1991).

16. Ewing v. California, 538 U.S. 11 (2003).

17. Federal Bureau of Prisons, "An Overview of the First Step Act," www
.bop.gov/inmates/fsa/overview.jsp.

18. William W. Berry II, "Extraordinary and Compelling: A Re-
Examination of the Justifications for Compassionate Release," *Maryland
Law Review* 68, no. 4 (2009): 861–62.

19. Berry, "Extraordinary and Compelling," 862–63.

20. Berry, "Extraordinary and Compelling," 868–69.

21. United States Sentencing Commission, "Guidelines Manual,
§3E1.1," November 2007. The history of compassionate release prior to
the First Step Act is recounted in United States v. Brooker, 976 F.3d 228
(2d Cir. 2020).

22. United States Sentencing Commission, "Sentencing Guidelines
for United States Courts," *Code of Federal Regulations*, 81 FR 27,261,
27,263-64 (2016), www.federalregister.gov/documents/2016/05/05/2016
-10431/sentencing-guidelines-for-united-states-courts.

23. United States Sentencing Commission, "Guidelines Manual §3E1.1,"
November 2018.

24. United States v. Brooker, 976 F.3d 228, 234 (2020).

25. Statement of Erica Zunkel, Clinical Professor of Law and Associate
Director, University of Chicago Law School's Federal Criminal Justice
Clinic, Before the United States Sentencing Commission Public Hearing on Proposed Amendments to Compassionate Release Policy Statement, February 23, 2023, www.ussc.gov/sites/default/files/pdf/amendment
-process/public-hearings-and-meetings/20230223-24/Zunkel.pdf.

26. *Brooker*, 976 F.3d 228.

27. United States v. Booker, 543 U.S. 220 (2005).

28. *Brooker*, 976 F.3d 228, 237.

29. United States v. Watts, 519 U.S. 148, 154 (1997).

30. Williams v. People of State of New York, 337 U.S. 241 (1949).

31. Death Penalty Information Center, "Jurors, Judges Urge Supreme Court to End Judicial Override of Life Sentences in Death Penalty Cases," November 19, 2020, deathpenaltyinfo.org/news/jurors-judges -urge-supreme-court-to-end-judicial-override-of-life-sentences-in-death -penalty-cases.

32. Meghann L. Lamb, "Overturning Override: Why Executing a Person Sentenced to Death by Judicial Override Violates the Eighth Amendment," *Southern California Law Review* 95, no. 3 (2022): 663.

33. Paige Williams, "Double Jeopardy," *New Yorker*, November 10, 2014.

34. These facts are recounted in my opinion in United States v. Fitch, 659 F.3d 788 (9th Cir. 2011).

35. *Fitch*, 659 F.3d 788.

36. United States Sentencing Commission, "Amendments to the Sentencing Guidelines," April 27, 2023, www.ussc.gov/sites/default/files/pdf /amendment-process/official-text-amendments/202305_Amendments .pdf.

8. Justin Volpe

1. 18 U.S.C. §3582(c)(1)(A) provides for two grounds for sentence modification: if (1) extraordinary and compelling reasons warrant reduction or (2) if "the defendant is at least 70 years of age, has served at least 30 years in prison, pursuant to a sentence imposed under section 3559(c), for the offense or offenses for which the defendant is currently imprisoned, and a determination has been made by the Director of the Bureau of Prisons that the defendant is not a danger to the safety of any other person or the community." This statutory, age-based ground for release is distinct from the age-based category the Sentencing Commission added as an extraordinary and compelling basis for sentence reduction to the Guidelines in

2016, which is discussed on pages 97 and 141. For the age-based ground, the Guidelines provide that extraordinary and compelling circumstances exist where "[t]he defendant (A) is at least 65 years old; (B) is experiencing a serious deterioration in physical or mental health because of the aging process; and (C) has served at least 10 years or 75 percent of his or her term of imprisonment, whichever is less." United States Sentencing Commission, "Guidelines Manual §1B1.13," November 2023.

2. Gregory P. Mango and Steve Janoski, "Disgraced Ex-cop Justin Volpe Says He Has 'Nothing But Love' for Victim Abner Louima After Being Released Early from Prison," *New York Post*, June 13, 2023.

3. Noah Goldberg, "'21 Years Is Not 21 Days': Abner Louima Says He Forgives, But Doesn't Forget, as NYPD Officer Who Sodomized Him Asks for Early Release from Prison," *New York Daily News*, January 5, 2021.

9. Sherwin Birkett

1. The canons are available at U.S. Courts, "Code of Conduct for United States Judges," www.uscourts.gov/judges-judgeships/code-conduct-united-states-judges.

2. *Ibid.*

3. David B. Rivkin Jr. and James Taranto, "Samuel Alito, the Supreme Court's Plain-Spoken Defender," *Wall Street Journal*, July 28, 2023.

4. Josh Gerstein, "Kagan Enters Fray over Congress' Power to Police Supreme Court," *Politico*, August 3, 2023, www.politico.com/news/2023/08/03/kagan-enters-fray-over-congress-power-to-police-supreme-court-00109770#:~:text=%E2%80%9COf%20course%2C%20Congress%20can%20regulate,the%20court's%20structure%20and%20composition.

5. Mark Sherman, "Chief Justice Roberts Says Supreme Court Can Do More on Ethics, But Offers No Specifics," Associated Press, May 24, 2023, apnews.com/article/supreme-court-john-roberts-ethics-5a3a356831e418140a7da78624718ef6.

6. Gerstein, "Kagan Enters Fray."

7. The preceding discussion is drawn from Adam Liptak, "Supreme Court's New Ethics Code Is Toothless, Experts Say," *New York Times*, November 14, 2023.

8. This discussion is drawn from my opinion in United States v. Birkett, No. 90-CR-1063-24, 2023 WL 4274683 (E.D.N.Y. June 29, 2023).

9. Issie Lapowsky, "Sentenced to Life as Boys, They Made Their Case for Release," *New York Times*, August 15, 2023.

10. Roper v. Simmons, 543 U.S. 551 (2005).

11. Lapowsky, "Sentenced to Life as Boys."

12. World Health Organization, "WHO Awards Countries for Progress in Eliminating Industrially Produced Trans Fats for First Time," (January 29, 2024), www.who.int/news/item/29-01-2024-who-awards-countries-for-progress-in-eliminating-industrially-produced-trans-fats-for-first-time#:~:text=While%20the%20ambitious%20target%20set,every%20region%20of%20the%20world.

13. Hawkins v. Kroger Co., 906 F.3d 763 (9th Cir. 2018).

14. Lapowsky, "Sentenced to Life."

15. Rob Abruzzese, "Lifetime in Prison to Freedom: Brooklyn Judge Frederic Block Grants Historic Release Under First Step Act," *Brooklyn Daily Eagle*, June 29, 2023, brooklyneagle.com/articles/2023/06/29/lifetime-in-prison-to-freedom-brooklyn-judge-frederic-block-grants-historic-release-under-first-step-act.

11. The Mafia Cases: Anthony Russo

1. United States v. Russo, No. 90-CR-1063, 2022 WL 16627450 (E.D.N.Y. Nov. 2, 2022). I issued an opinion amending and superseding the November 2 decision on November 28. United States v. Russo, 643 F. Supp. 3d 325 (E.D.N.Y. 2022).

2. Luc Cohen, "Bankman-Fried Heads to Brooklyn Jail Notorious for Poor Conditions," Reuters, August 14, 2023.

3. Annie Correal and Joseph Goldstein, "'It's Cold as Hell': Inside a Brooklyn Jail's Weeklong Collapse," *New York Times*, February 9, 2019.

4. Cohen, "Bankman-Fried Heads to Brooklyn Jail."

5. John Marzulli, "Exclusive: Judge Refuses to Send Women to Brooklyn Jail with 'Third World' Conditions," *New York Daily News*, October 7, 2016.

6. Benjamin Weiser, "Judge Refuses to Send Defendant in Drug Case to Troubled Brooklyn Jail," *New York Times*, January 4, 2024.

7. New York City Comptroller, "The State of New York City Jails," August 2023, comptroller.nyc.gov/wp-content/uploads/documents/The-State-of-New-York-City-Jails.pdf.

8. The Vera Institute reports that "[s]ixty percent of the people in New York City's jails who have lost a year or more of their lives to pretrial detention are Black, even though Black people make up only about 24 percent of New York City's population." Nicholas Turner, "Waiting to Go to Court Shouldn't Be a Death Sentence," Vera Institute, March 18, 2022, www.vera.org/news/waiting-to-go-to-court-shouldnt-be-a-death-sentence.

9. Jan Ransom and Jonah E. Bromwich, "Tracking the Deaths in New York City's Jail System," *New York Times*, October 19, 2023.

10. United States v. Russo, No. 90-CR-1063, 2022. I issued an opinion amending and superseding the November 2 decision on November 28. United States v. Russo, 643 F. Supp. 3d 325 (E.D.N.Y. 2022).

11. The online version of this article is available at John Annese, "Mobster and Drug Gang Killer Ordered Released by Federal Judge: 'I Am Letting Two Murderers Sentenced to Life Out of Prison,'" *New York Daily News*, November 2, 2022.

12. Frederic Block, "A Slow Death," *New York Times*, March 15, 2007.

12. The Mafia Cases: Vittorio "Little Vic" Amuso

1. Danielle Wallace, "Former Mafia Boss Vittorio Amuso, 88, Convicted of Ordering Several Murders Pleads for 'Compassionate Release' from Prison," *New York Post*, June 21, 2023.

2. My opinion is at United States v. Amuso, No. 90-CR-00446, 2023 WL 5153425 (E.D.N.Y. Aug. 10, 2023).

3. John Annese, "Lucchese Mob Boss Vic Amuso 'Too Destructive to Society' to Get Early Prison Release, Judge Says," *New York Daily News*, August 10, 2023.

4. Bruce Golding, "Judge Denies 'Compassionate Release' for NYC Mafia Godfather, 88, Who Ordered 12 Murders," *The Messenger*, August 10, 2023, themessenger.com/news/judge-denies-compassionate -release-for-nyc-mafia-godfather-88-who-ordered-12-murders.

5. Katie Engelhart, "I've Reported on Dementia for Years, and One Image of a Prisoner Keeps Haunting Me," *New York Times*, August 11, 2023.

6. Ben Austen, *Correction: Parole, Prison, and the Possibility of Change* (New York: Flatiron Books, 2023), 23.

7. Austen, 23.

13. The Mafia Cases: Anthony "Gaspipe" Casso

1. Priscilla DeGregory, Larry Celona, and Tamar Lapin, "Ex-Lucchese Underboss Anthony 'Gaspipe' Casso Dies After Getting COVID-19 in Prison," *New York Post*, December 16, 2020.

2. Ashley Nellis and Liz Komar, "The First Step Act: Ending Mass Incarceration in Federal Prisons," The Sentencing Project, August 22, 2023, www.sentencingproject.org/policy-brief/the-first-step-act-ending -mass-incarceration-in-federal-prisons.

14. The Next Step

1. May v. Shinn, 954 F.3d 1194 (9th Cir. 2020).

2. May v. Shinn, 37 F.4th 552 (9th Cir. 2022), cert. denied sub nom. May v. Thornell, 143 S. Ct. 789 (2023).

3. Arizona State Senate Issue Brief, "Truth in Sentencing," August 3, 2018, www.azleg.gov/Briefs/Senate/TRUTH%20IN%20 SENTENCING%202018.pdf.

4. Jeremy Duda, "Ducey Vetoes 'Repeat Offender' Bill, But Signs Measure to Ease Sentences for Some Drug Offenders," *Arizona Mirror*, June 7, 2019, www.azmirror.com/2019/06/07/ducey-vetoes-repeat-offender-bill -but-signs-measure-to-ease-sentences-for-some-drug-offenders.

5. Arizona State Senate Issue Brief, "Truth in Sentencing."

6. Jorge Renaud, "Grading the Parole Release Systems of All 50 States," *Prison Policy Initiative*, February 26, 2019, www.prisonpolicy.org/reports/grading_parole.html.

7. *May*, 954 F.3d at 1208-09 (Friedland, J., concurring).

8. Renaud, "Grading."

9. Ralph Chapoco, "Report: Alabama Parole Grants Fall to 7%," *Alabama Reflector*, September 21, 2023, alabamareflector.com/2023/09/21/report-alabama-parole-grants-fall-to-7.

10. Death Penalty Information Center, "Innocence," deathpenaltyinfo.org/policy-issues/innocence.

11. National Institute of Justice, "Wrongful Convictions: The Literature, the Issues, and the Unheard Voices," December 2023, 43, www.ojp.gov/pdffiles1/nij/251446.pdf.

12. Georgia Innocence Project, "Beneath the Statistics: The Structural and Systemic Causes of Our Wrongful Conviction Problem," www.georgiainnocenceproject.org/general/beneath-the-statistics-the-structural-and-systemic-causes-of-our-wrongful-conviction-problem.

13. The Innocence Project, "About," innocenceproject.org/about/.

14. The National Registry of Exonerations, "Exoneration Registry," www.law.umich.edu/special/exoneration/Pages/detaillist.aspx.

15. Collins v. City of New York, 923 F. Supp. 2d 462 (E.D.N.Y. 2013).

16. The City of New York, "Mayor Adams Announces Three Appointments to Commission to Combat Police Corruption," May 30, 2023, www.nyc.gov/office-of-the-mayor/news/372-23/mayor-adams-three-appointments-commission-combat-police-corruption.

17. "Post-Conviction Justice Bureau." The Brooklyn District Attorney's Office, http://www.brooklynda.org/post-conviction-justicebureau/.

18. Frederic Block, "Let's Put an End to Prosecutorial Immunity," Marshall Project, March 13, 2018, www.themarshallproject.org/2018/03/13/let-s-put-an-end-to-prosecutorial-immunity.

19. Frederic Block, "Prosecutors Aren't Above the Law: Gov. Cuomo Must Sign Legislation Creating an Oversight Commission," *New York Daily News*, July 30, 2018.

20. New York State Government, "New York State Commission on Prosecutorial Conduct," www.ny.gov/new-york-state-commission-prosecutorial-conduct.

21. The following bullet points are quoted from National Registry of Exonerations, "Government Misconduct and Convicting the Innocent: The Role of Prosecutors, Police and Other Law Enforcement," September 1, 2020, www.law.umich.edu/special/exoneration/Documents/Government_Misconduct_and_Convicting_the_Innocent.pdf.

22. National Registry of Exonerations, "2022 Annual Report," May 8, 2023, 7–12.

23. The National Registry of Exonerations, "25,000 Years Lost to Wrongful Convictions," June 14, 2021, 4.

24. May v. Shinn, 37 F.4th 552, 562 (9th Cir. 2022).

Postscript: Collateral Consequences

1. Michelle Alexander, *The New Jim Crow: Mass Incarceration in the Age of Colorblindness* (The New Press, 2012), 141.

2. United States v. Nesbeth, 188 F. Supp. 3d 179 (E.D.N.Y. 2016).

3. Post Editorial Board, "Brooklyn Judge Attempts to Rewrite Laws with an Outrageous Wrist-Slap for Drug Felon," *New York Post*, May 25, 2016.

4. Benjamin Weiser, "U.S. Judge's Striking Move in Felony Drug Case: Probation, Not Prison," *New York Times*, May 25, 2016.

5. Adam Chandler, "Paying (and Paying and Paying) a Debt to Society," *The Atlantic*, May 31, 2016.

6. Lincoln Caplan, "Why a Brooklyn Judge Refused to Send a Drug Courier to Prison," *New Yorker*, June 1, 2016.

7. Leon Neyfakh, "In a Remarkable Decision, Federal Judge Lays Out All the Ways Our Justice System Hurts Ex-Cons," *Slate*, May 25, 2016, slate.com/news-and-politics/2016/05/frederic-block-federal-judge-speaks-out-against-collateral-consequences-for-felons.html.

8. John Malcolm, "Being an Ex-offender Is Tough Enough," Heritage Foundation, February 14, 2018, www.heritage.org/crime-and-justice/commentary/being-ex-offender-tough-enough.

9. Clean Slate Initiative, "Clean Slate in the States," www
.cleanslateinitiative.org/states#states.

10. Collateral Consequences Resource Center, "The Frontiers of Dignity:
Clean Slate and Other Criminal Record Reforms in 2022," January 10,
2023, ccresourcecenter.org/2023/01/10/the-frontiers-of-dignity-clean
-slate-and-other-criminal-record-reforms-in-2022.

11. The Collateral Consequences Resource Center reports that these
states and the District of Columbia "enacted no fewer than 37 laws limiting
disenfranchisement or encouraging the newly enfranchised to vote, with
additional executive orders and ballot initiatives." Margaret Colgate Love,
"The Many Roads from Reentry to Reintegration: A National Survey of
Laws Restoring Rights and Opportunities After Arrest or Conviction,"
Collateral Consequences Resource Center, March 2022, ccresourcecenter
.org/the-many-roads-to-reintegration.

12. Brennan Center, "A Federal Agenda for Criminal Justice Reform,"
December 9, 2020, www.brennancenter.org/our-work/policy-solutions
/federal-agenda-criminal-justice-reform.

13. Clean Slate Initiative, "It's Time for a Federal Clean Slate," www
.cleanslateinitiative.org/federal.

14. Federal Register, "Veteran-Owned Small Business and Service-
Disabled Veteran-Owned Small Business-Certification," November 29,
2022, www.federalregister.gov/documents/2022/11/29/2022-25508
/veteran-owned-small-business-and-service-disabled-veteran-owned
-small-business-certification.

15. The White House, "Statement from President Biden on Marijuana Reform," October 6, 2022, www.whitehouse.gov/briefing-room
/statements-releases/2022/10/06/statement-from-president-biden-on
-marijuana-reform/#:~:text=There%20are%20thousands%20of%20
people,consequences%20arising%20from%20these%20convictions.

Epilogue

1. Deal v. United States, 508 U.S. 129 (1993).

2. United States v. Sessoms, 565 F. Supp. 3d 325 (E.D.N.Y. 2021).

3. United States v. Weir, 2:10-cr-00007-JMS-CMM-27, (S.D. Ind. Oct. 3, 2023).

4. United States v. Cromitie, No. 09 CR 558-01 (CM), 2024 WL 216540 (S.D.N.Y. Jan. 19, 2024).

ABOUT THE AUTHOR

Frederic Block is a U.S. district court judge for the Eastern District of New York. He has been at the forefront of releasing prisoners and has received both praise and grief in the media. Judge Block is the author of several books, including his memoir *Disrobed* and the reality-fiction novel *Race to Judgment*, the basis for an incipient TV series. He lives in New York City.

PUBLISHING IN THE PUBLIC INTEREST

Thank you for reading this book published by The New Press; we hope you enjoyed it. New Press books and authors play a crucial role in sparking conversations about the key political and social issues of our day.

We hope that you will stay in touch with us. Here are a few ways to keep up to date with our books, events, and the issues we cover:

- Sign up at www.thenewpress.com/subscribe to receive updates on New Press authors and issues and to be notified about local events
- www.facebook.com/newpressbooks
- www.twitter.com/thenewpress
- www.instagram.com/thenewpress

Please consider buying New Press books not only for yourself, but also for friends and family and to donate to schools, libraries, community centers, prison libraries, and other organizations involved with the issues our authors write about.

The New Press is a 501(c)(3) nonprofit organization; if you wish to support our work with a tax-deductible gift please visit www.thenewpress.com/donate or use the QR code below.